INSIGHT ⊙ GUIDES

D0522853

VIENNA
POCKET GUIDE

www.insightguides.com/Austria

◉ Walking Eye App

Your Insight Pocket Guide purchase includes a free download of the destination's corresponding eBook. It is available now from the free Walking Eye container app in the App Store and Google Play. Simply download the Walking Eye container app to access the eBook dedicated to your purchased book. The app also features free information on local events taking place and activities you can enjoy during your stay, with the option to book them. In addition, premium content for a wide range of other destinations is available to purchase in-app.

HOW TO DOWNLOAD THE WALKING EYE APP

Available on purchase of this guide only.
1. Visit our website: www.insightguides.com/walkingeye
2. Download the Walking Eye container app to your smartphone (this will give you access to your free eBook and the ability to purchase other products)
3. Select the scanning module in the Walking Eye container app
4. Scan the QR Code on this page – you will be asked to enter a verification word from the book as proof of purchase
5. Download your free eBook* for travel information on the go

*Other destination apps and eBooks are available for purchase separately or are free with the purchase of the Insight Guide book

TOP 10 ATTRACTIONS

SCHÖNBRUNN
Empress Maria Theresa's opulent rococo palace and gardens. See page 66.

STEPHANSDOM
The cathedral at the heart of Vienna's Innere Stadt. See page 27.

DER·ZEIT·IHRE·KVNST
DER·KVNST·IHRE·FREIHEIT

THE SECESSION BUILDING
Home to Gustav Klimt's 34m (1 ft) long *Beethoven Frieze*. See page 55.

KUNSTHISTORISCHES MUSEUM
Works by Raphael are among its many masterpieces. See page 51.

KARLSPLATZ
It has numerous attractions in addition to the Karlskirche. See page 56.

THE SPANISH RIDING SCHOOL
See the Lipizzaner stallions perform. See page 44.

THE BELVEDERE
Among its treasures is Klimt's *The Kiss*. See page 60.

THE HOFBURG
Imperial palace of the Habsburgs. See page 42.

THE MUSEUMSQUARTIER
Where the Museum of Modern Art, Architecture Centre and multimedia exhibitions can all be found. See page 53.

THE PRATER
Vienna's huge expanse of parkland, home to the Riesenrad. See page 70.

A PERFECT DAY

9.00am

Breakfast
A hearty Alpine breakfast is a great set-up for the day, so eat your fill either from your hotel buffet or from the diet-busting breakfast menu at Café Drechsler (see page 109).

12 noon

Lunch
Take your midday pangs to tiny Immervoll (see page 105) for some authentic Viennese fare in the company of the city's office workers, or Trzesniewski (see page 105) for a traditional open sandwich with lunchtime diners on the hop.

1.00pm

10.00am

Royal Palace
Kick off your day of sightseeing at the Stephansdom with great city views from the tower; then take the U-Bahn southwest to Schloss Schönnbrunn, the Habsburg's baroque masterpiece. You'll just have time to take a tour of the 40 dazzling rooms before returning to the city centre.

Museum visit
After lunch take the U-Bahn or tram to the famous Museums-Quartier. MUMOK and Leopold Museum are top choices, and across the road stands the superb Kunst-historisches Museum. Cafés are plentiful too if you need to refuel.

8.30pm

Tavern time

A great way to round off the day is to head out of town to a *Heuriger* (wine tavern), perhaps Braunsperger (see page 107) or Fuhrgassl-Huber (see page 108) to sip some excellent local reds and whites as well as traditional food. They're easily accessible from the city centre.

5.00pm

Mine's a *Beisl*

Taking an early dinner frees up the rest of the evening for more Viennese experiences, so make your way to one of the city's friendly *Beisln*, a type of informal bistro with authentic local food. Beim Czaak (see page 103) or Reinthaler (see page 105) are popular with inner-city dwellers.

3.30pm

Take a break

Time to take a break, so hop across from the museum action into the Volksgarten for a quiet stroll, perhaps stopping off for a coffee at an open-air café.

6.30pm

In a spin

Next stop is the Prater amusement park for a spin on the big wheel, the Riesenrad, immortalised in the film *The Third Man*. If fun fairs are not your thing, there are plenty of Danube-side walks to take and parkland to explore, perhaps by bike.

CONTENTS

INTRODUCTION

The sophisticated Viennese enjoy what is known as the *Wiener Lebensart*, a cultured appreciation of all life's pleasures. Not only is this reflected in Vienna's glorious art, music and architecture, theatres and coffee houses, and its passion for glittering balls, but where else would you find vineyards within a city's limits? The Innere Stadt (Old City) is a Unesco World Heritage Site (in addition to the Schloss Schönbrunn), a fitting honour for an area that embraces baroque palaces, the famous Burgtheater and Staatsoper (Opera House), and a warren of narrow medieval streets and lanes tangled around the Stephansdom (St Stephen's Cathedral).

Yet Vienna, with a population of 1.8 million, has much to save it from becoming an open-air museum. Tired old sites are regularly revamped and given new uses, and various construction projects, from the whimsy of Hundertwasser's garbage incinerator to the steel Millennium Tower, add a 21st-century dimension. In the historic centre, projects such as the MuseumsQuartier blend old and new to bring fresh interest to the Austrian capital's cityscape. Vienna is divided into 23 districts. The 1st District is the historic Innere Stadt (Old City), and districts 2 to 9 fan out around the Ringstrasse.

Viennese charm

The Viennese seldom miss an opportunity to make a flattering remark: 'I kiss your hand, Madam' or 'I am honoured'. Even the familiar greeting *Servus* ('hi' or 'bye') is Latin for 'your servant'.

Since the 16th century, Vienna has been universally acknowledged as Europe's capital of music. People come here to enjoy the waltzes of Johann Strauss – only he could have described the muddy brown Danube as blue

Aerial view of the city at night

– and baroque Mozart recitals at the Opera House. Visit the *Heuriger* wine garden on the edge of the Vienna Woods (Wienerwald) for a late-night glass of white wine and a few sentimental songs or knock back a couple of beers to something more modern in one of the city's clubs. And when all you want to do is kick back, Vienna is a city with plenty of space to relax in, its rural setting inducing an easy-going attitude to life.

TRADITION AND MODERNITY

The Viennese are proud of their city's heritage and are great at achieving both continuity and change in equal measure. Grand old hotels and coffee houses have been symapthetically renovated, and the clientele – the artists, writers, thinkers and dreamers – have been joined by media moguls, bankers and business professionals, and of course tourists too. Fashion designers have taken hold of the traditional *Loden* fabric and produced it in brighter hues to give a bit of oomph to the traditional olive-green jackets and overcoats, while the revered Burgtheater is constantly challenging opinions with provocative productions by the likes of Thomas Bernhard.

The Austrian capital also offers an astonishing range of museums, from the sublime to the surprising, from art and high culture to schnapps and reusable coffins (many of these can be visited for free or at reduced rates with the Vienna Card, available from the tourist information office). But some things don't change: *Fiakers* (carriages) still trundle tourists around the city centre; the pure white Lipizzaner stallions still prance at the Spanish Riding School; the Café Konditorei still lure customers with their creamy gateaux and the annual balls remain the focal point of the social calendar. The biggest event of the year however falls in May when the Life Ball brings hordes of

THE WALTZ

Music in Vienna is fuelled not only by its hallowed classical tradition, but also by the joy of its waltzes. The waltz began as a triple-time German traditional dance known as a *Ländler*, which the Viennese transformed into a whirling moment of fairyland. The man who brought the waltz to popular dance halls in 1819 was Joseph Lanner, leader of a small band. He took on a young viola player named Johann Strauss and the waltz took off in a big way. The group grew to become an orchestra and Strauss broke away to form his own – Lanner sadly celebrating the occasion with his *Trennungswalzer (Separation Waltz)*. The two conducted a prolonged 'waltz war' for public favour in the cafés of the Prater. The rivalry ended amicably and Strauss played waltzes – *adagio* – at Lanner's funeral.

celebrtities to the city and is Europe's largest AIDS charity event.

AT THE CROSSROADS

Vienna's historic role as a crossroads of Eastern and Western European civilisation has taken on a new significance since the collapse of Soviet communism and Austria's entry into the European Union in 1995. It's a veritable melting pot of cultures with a workforce made up of new generations of Poles, Italians, Turks, Croats and more.The city's relaxed atmosphere often

Urban transport

comes as a surprise to visitors and the Viennese still seem to have time for the courtesies of yesteryear. Although recent social innovations have been generally popular in Vienna, people remain profoundly conservative in their values. Politically the Viennese have always been impossible to define. They cheered their Habsburg emperors and then Napoleon. They welcomed the republican experiment after World War I, hailed Hitler, then found democracy rather to their liking as it seemed conducive to their legendary taste for *Gemütlichkeit*. Roughly translated, *gemütlich* means 'comfy and cosy', the quality that takes the rough edges off life. It is part of the famous Viennese charm, a charm also sharpened by undertones of sometimes malicious irony known as *Wiener Schmäh* (Viennese sarcasm).

A BRIEF HISTORY

From earliest times, Vienna was a crossroads for people migrating between Eastern and Western Europe. The first identifiable inhabitants of the area were Illyrians who sailed up the Danube from the Balkan Peninsula. Celts migrating from Gaul founded the town of Vindobona ('Shining Field') around 500BC.

ROMANS AND BARBARIANS

The Romans arrived in the 1st century AD. Dispatched from Britain to shore up the empire's eastern European frontier, Rome's soldiers built their garrison in what is today the Inner City's Hoher Markt. They had their work cut out fending off invasions from the Teutons and Slavs. Emperor Marcus Aurelius led the fight against the barbarians, but died in Vindobona of the plague in AD180. A hundred years later, another Roman emperor, Probus, won the gratitude of subsequent generations by establishing vineyards on the slopes of the Wienerwald. Today, Probusgasse, a street in the heart of the *Heuriger* wine district of Heiligenstadt, honours his initiative.

Christianity arrived in the 4th century, but was powerless against successive waves of barbarian warriors. Attila the Hun advanced on Vienna in 453, but died before completing his conquest. The Huns were followed over the next 600 years by rampaging Goths, Franks, Avars, Slavs and Magyars. Despite these troubles, the first church, Ruprechtskirche, was erected in 740. Two more followed during the reign of Charlemagne: Maria am Gestade and the Peterskirche.

BABENBERG RULE

Stability came in 1156 when the Babenbergs, Bavarian lords who had succeeded a century and a half earlier in driving out the Magyars, were granted the hereditary duchy of Austria by the Holy Roman Emperor.

The first duke, Heinrich II Jasomirgott, set up his court around what is today the Platz am Hof, giving Vienna its first golden era. Art, trade and handicrafts thrived, attracting immigrant German merchants and artisans. Vienna became an important stopover for crusaders. Scottish and Irish monks on their way to Jerusalem founded the monastery of Schottenstift. Babenberg rule brought many new churches, notably the first Stephansdom, as well as several monasteries, elegant residences for the nobility along the broad new thoroughfares, and a fortress on the site of the future Hofburg castle. In 1200, financed with English ransom money paid to liberate King Richard the Lion Heart, a ring of fortifications was built around the Innere Stadt, along what is now the Ringstrasse. It was also the great era of the minstrels and the start of Vienna's long musical tradition.

Babenberg family tree at the monastery of Klosterneuburg

THE HABSBURGS

In 1246, on the death of Friedrich der Streitbare (the Quarrelsome), the male line of the Babenbergs died out and the country fell to Ottokar II of Bohemia. Unlike his predecessor, who had disturbed the city's hard-earned peace by picking fights with his barons, seducing the burghers' wives and going

Obscure origins

For a dynasty that was to supply rulers to Germany, Austria, Hungary, Bohemia, Spain and other states, the Habsburgs had obscure origins. The house took its name from the castle of Habsburg, or Habichtsburg (Hawk's Castle), on the Aar River in present-day Switzerland, built by Werner, Bishop of Strasbourg, and his brother Count Radbot.

off to war at the slightest provocation, Ottokar was popular with the Viennese. He made additions to the Stephansdom and started on the Hofburg. The people did not seem to appreciate that the new German king, Rudolf von Habsburg, had his eye on the city. They supported Ottokar, but in 1278 Rudolf triumphed.

Vienna's history for centuries thereafter was about constant confrontation between the Habsburgs' visions of grandeur and world conquest and the citizens' taste for the quiet life. Whenever the Habsburgs went about their empire-building, under Maximilian I, Karl V and Ferdinand I, Vienna was painfully neglected. The most popular rulers were the ones who chose to stay home and build things. Rudolf der Stifter (the Founder) created the university in 1365 and turned the Romanesque Stephansdom into the Gothic masterpiece you see today. Friedrich III finished the job and won Rome's approval for Vienna to become a bishopric in 1469. The Viennese showed their appreciation by burying him in the cathedral. As his tomb attests, it was Friedrich who dreamed up the grandiose motto: AEIOU, *'Austriae Est Imperare Orbi Universo'*, for which the English translation is 'It falls to Austria to rule the world'.

The 15th century was not all sweetness and light: in 1421, more than 200 Jews were burned alive in their quarter around Judenplatz and the remainder were driven out of the city. The Hungarian king Matthias Corvinus occupied Vienna from 1485 to 1490. He is remembered for his remark: 'Let others wage war while you, happy Austria, arrange marriages. What Mars gives to others, you receive from Venus.' The reference was to the Habsburgs' knack of expanding their empire through judicious mating of their innumerable archdukes and archduchesses, a policy that was used to great advantage by Maximilian I (1493–1519).

Picking up where the Goths and the Magyars left off, the Ottomans under Suleiman the Magnificent staged a crippling 18-day siege of Vienna in 1529. The suburbs were devastated, but the Innere Stadt held fast and the Turks were finally forced to retreat.

In the Reformation of the 16th century and the Thirty Years War that followed, the city emerged as a bulwark of the Catholic Church. Having withstood the Muslim Turks, Vienna banned Protestant worship in 1577, and repelled an attack by the Protestant Swedes of Gustav Adolph in 1645.

Close-up of the Hofburg Imperial Palace

Jews were allowed back into town, having been confined during the 1620s to a ghetto on the riverside marshlands of Leopoldstadt. Emperor Leopold I was the one to usher Vienna into its glorious baroque era, a feast of architecture and music that scarcely paused to deal with the vicious plague of 1679 and another Ottoman siege in 1683. The great soldier and scholar Prince Eugene of Savoy was rewarded for his victory over the Turks with ample funds to build the magnificent and now renowned Belvedere Palace. The Auerspergs, Schwarzenbergs and Liechtensteins followed suit with palaces of a more modest, but equally elegant variety.

Karl VI, pretender to the Spanish throne, returned to Vienna more Spanish than Austrian, bringing with him the strict formality and piety of the Spanish court. His renovation of the 12th-century Abbey Klosterneuburg in baroque style was an attempt to create an Austrian version of El Escorial. Similarly, the huge Karlskirche was originally intended to emulate St Peter's in Rome. Vying with Versailles, the Hofburg Palace built the Spanish Riding School and the Imperial Library. The transformation of Vienna into a baroque city was largely the work of three Austrian architects: Johann Bernhard Fischer von Erlach, his son Josef Emanuel, and Johann Lukas von Hildebrandt.

PRINCE EUGENE OF SAVOY (1663–1736)

Sceptical by nature, the Viennese have few authentic heroes; ironically, the greatest was a Frenchman who became the supreme Austrian patriot. A unique blend of military courage, culture and human warmth, Prince Eugene of Savoy was born in Paris in 1663. He arrived in Vienna in 1683, just in time to help out with the campaigns against the Turks. Over the next 30 years he fought brilliantly for Austria against the Ottomans and the French, rising to the position of commander-in-chief in 1697. Small of stature and always dressed in a simple brown uniform, he was known to his soldiers as 'the little Capuchin'.

MARIA THERESA AND NAPOLEON

Empress Maria Theresa

After the feverish construction projects that crowned the empire-building efforts of the male Habsburgs, the Viennese were delighted to be able to relax under the maternal eye of Empress Maria Theresa (1740–80). Pious, warm and sentimental, this mother of 16 children had an unerring feel for the moods of her capital's citizens. She was an enthusiastic patron of the arts, especially music. She loved to have concerts and operas performed at her newly completed Schönbrunn Palace, which she infinitely preferred to the more austere Hofburg. Her orchestra director was Christoph Gluck, a young Joseph Haydn sang in the Vienna Boys' Choir, and six-year-old Wolfgang Amadeus Mozart won Maria Theresa's heart by asking for the hand of one of her daughters (as fate would have it, the daughter in question, Marie-Antoinette, was destined to lose her head for somebody else). In the following years, these three composers – Gluck, Haydn and Mozart – launched Vienna's reputation as a city of music.

Whatever her virtues, it must be said that Maria Theresa lulled the Viennese into a false sense of security. Her son Joseph II (1780–90), very serious-minded and not particularly tactful, shocked them into a reluctant awareness of the revolutionary times that were coming. He rushed through a series of far-reaching reforms, making life easier for peasants, Protestants and Jews. But the conservative Viennese were

Famous faces

Psychoanalyst Sigmund Freud, composer Gustav Mahler and playwright Arthur Schnitzler were all famous Viennese residents.

not ready. They were startled to see him open up the city by tearing down the wall around the Innere Stadt, and were dumbfounded by the bureaucratic machine he installed to run the empire.

People felt more secure with the cynical and not at all reform-minded Franz II, particularly following the news from France of the execution of Joseph's sister Marie-Antoinette. On seeing the strange tricolour flag hoisted by the new envoy of the French republic, the Viennese promptly tore it to shreds – along with diplomatic relations between Austria and France. They were less bumptious when Napoleon's armies arrived in November 1805 and the French emperor moved into Maria Theresa's Schönbrunn on his way to further glories at Austerlitz (in Moravia to the north).

Once more, the Habsburgs' secret weapon in foreign policy, politically astute marriages, came into play. Now, faced in 1810 with saving what was left of the empire, Emperor Franz did not hesitate to give his daughter Marie-Louise in marriage to his enemy Napoleon. The Viennese did not protest, preferring a peaceful life to more war.

THE LONG 19TH CENTURY

The Napoleonic era ended with one of the city's most splendid moments, the Congress of Vienna in 1815, organised by Franz's shrewd chancellor, Metternich, for the post-war carving up of Napoleon's Europe. Franz was happy to leave the diplomatic shenanigans to Metternich while he supervised a non-stop spectacle of banquets, balls and concerts. Many considered Franz more successful than Metternich. 'This Congress does not make progress,' said Belgium's Prince de Ligne, 'it dances.'

For the next 30 years or so the city relaxed for a period of gracious living for the middle class and aristocracy, with the Prater park a favourite outing for royalty. And it was time for more music; Beethoven had become the darling of an aristocracy eager to make amends for its shameful neglect of Mozart. But in general the taste was more for the waltzes of Johann Strauss, both father and son.

In 1848 Vienna became caught up in a wave of revolution that spread across Europe in support of national independence and political reform. Ferdinand, the most sweet-natured but also the most dimwitted of Habsburg emperors, exclaimed when he heard that disgruntled citizens were marching on his Hofburg, 'Are they allowed to do that?' He fled town before getting an answer. The authoritarian Metternich was forced out of power, and the mob hanged the war minister, Theodor Latour, from a lamp post before imperial troops brutally re-established order.

Johann Strauss the Younger commemorated in the Stadtpark

Emperor Franz Joseph

Ferdinand abdicated and his deadly earnest nephew, Franz Joseph, took over. Grimly aware of his enormous burden, Franz Joseph concentrated throughout his 68-year reign on defending his family's interests and preserving as much of the empire as possible. Vienna offered him a paradoxically triumphant arena in which to preside over inevitable imperial decline. Prospering from the Industrial Revolution, the city enthusiastically developed the Ringstrasse, with imposing residences for capitalism's new aristocracy and expanded residential districts for the burgeoning bourgeoisie.

The World Fair in 1873, which nearly bankrupted the city, sang its praises, and people travelled from Europe and America to see the new opera house, concert halls and theatres. To a soundtrack by Brahms, Bruckner, Mahler, Lehar and Strauss the Austrian Empire's cultural achievements were consecrated in monumental form before the empire itself disintegrated. At the Secession Gallery, a group of young artists introduced a new style of art, which came to be known as *Jugendstil* (Art Nouveau). Only a spoilsport like Sigmund Freud over at the university would suggest that the Viennese examine the depths of their unconscious for the seeds of their darker impulses. They, of course, paid no attention. As the intellectuals in the coffee houses clucked disapprovingly, the town waltzed on. Meanwhile a would-be painter named Adolf Hitler quietly left town in disgust at this lack of seriousness, blaming the Jews and Slavs he had encountered in Vienna for the problems of the 'true Germans'.

THE END OF THE EMPIRE

Having lost his son Rudolf through a suicide in Mayerling, and his wife Elisabeth to an assassin's knife in Geneva, Franz Joseph was stricken but fatalistic when he heard that his heir, Archduke Franz Ferdinand, had been shot in Sarajevo. The World War (1914–18) that followed ended the Habsburg Empire and left Vienna in economic ruin. Vienna lost its hinterland of Bohemia, Moravia, Slovakia, Hungary, parts of Poland, Romania and what was Yugoslavia, all of which had brought it economic prosperity.

Following World War I the state opera could boast Richard Strauss as its director, and the old creative spirit re-emerged in architecturally progressive public housing but the city suffered from crippling inflation. Politically polarised, street fighting broke out between Communists and Fascist supporters of the government of Engelbert Dollfuss. In 1934 Dollfuss was assassinated by the outlawed Austrian Nazis in the Chancellery on Ballhausplatz. His successor, Kurt von Schuschnigg, succeeded in crushing the putsch, but was forced four years later to yield to Hitler's *Anschluss* (German annexation) of Austria.

On 13 March 1938, Hitler's triumphant drive along the Maria-hilferstrasse was cheered by the Viennese, who saw him as their saviour from the chaos of recent years. He proved the opposite for the city's 180,000 Jews. The brutality of the Austrian Nazis and the spite of many local citizens shocked even those who had

No trace

Hitler's residence in the city is not commemorated. It is recorded that he stayed in a hostel at Meldemannstrasse 27 and that he had a flat at Stumpergasse 31. But there isn't anything to see at either site.

witnessed their counterparts at work in Germany. The extermination of the Viennese Jews left a great stain on the city and a gaping hole in its intellectual life and cosmopolitan culture.

In some small measure, the city's spirit survived in World War II. Joseph Bürckel, the Nazi Gauleiter overseeing Vienna, warned Goebbels that it was perhaps better to allow satirical cabaret to continue. However, by the bombardments of 1945 all humour had evaporated. After the war, Vienna, like Berlin, was divided into four sectors, with the Innere Stadt under the joint administration of the Americans, Russians, British and French. The penury was countered by stoic acceptance and a vicious black market.

Austria's post-war neutrality, granted in 1955, made Vienna an appropriate host for the International Atomic Energy Agency, the United Nations Industrial Development Organisation and OPEC.

Austria joined the European Union in 1995, once more giving Vienna an active role in Europe. However, with the entry of a far-right party into the governing coalition, the country's reputation for unsavoury political attitudes again came under scrutiny, and the following years saw Austria enact some of the most restrictive immigration laws in the EU. The Viennese still cling firmly to their social-democratic traditions, but Austria is evenly split between left and right. The far right shows no sign of disappearing, even surviving the death of its populist leader Jörg Haider in a car crash in 2008. Following the 2013 legislative election a grand coalition government ('Grosse Koalition') was formed by the left-wing Social Democratic Party of Austria and the right-wing Austrian People's Party.

Modern Vienna's UNO-City

HISTORICAL LANDMARKS

c. 500 BC Celts build town of Vindobona.

1st century AD Romans establish garrison.

4th–9th century Barbarian invasions.

740 Ruprechtskirche is built, the earliest known Christian church.

1156–1246 Babenbergs reign as dukes of Vienna; the first Stephansdom cathedral and precursor of the Hofburg castle is built.

1278 Rudolf von Habsburg launches 640-year dynasty.

1365 University of Vienna founded.

1421 Jewish pogrom; 200 burned to death.

1529 First Turkish siege repelled.

1577 Catholic Church bans Reformation Protestants.

17th C Jews confined to ghetto and then allowed back into town.

1683 Second Turkish siege repelled.

1740–80 Popular Maria Theresa makes her home in Schönbrunn Palace; Haydn and Mozart make Vienna the musical capital.

1780–90 Joseph II's reforms prove unpopular with the Viennese.

1815 The Congress of Vienna carves up Europe while princes dance.

1848 Short-lived revolt drives Metternich from Vienna. Emperor Ferdinand replaced by Franz Joseph (1848–1916).

1873 World Fair celebrates Vienna's grandeur.

1900 Sigmund Freud writes *The Interpretation of Dreams*.

1914–18 Defeat in World War I ends Austrian Empire.

1934 Austrian Nazis assassinate Chancellor Dollfuss.

1938 German annexation (*Anschluss*) of Austria.

1939–45 World War II: Allied bombs devastate city.

1955 Austria granted neutrality.

1995 Austria enters European Union.

2005 Austria celebrates *Jubiläumsjahr*, the 50th anniversary of the State Treaty and 60th of the Second Republic.

2013 Coalition government formed with the Social Democratic Party of Austria and the Austrian People's Party.

2015 New laws ban foreign funding for mosques and imams.

2016 Vienna voted the most liveable city in the world (Mercer survey).

WHERE TO GO

Nearly all Vienna's major attractions are packed into the Innere Stadt (Inner City). This means that places such as the Stephansdom (St Stephen's Cathedral), the Hofburg (Imperial Palace), the Burgtheater (National Theatre), Mozart's house, the Staatsoper (State Opera) and the shopping areas around Kärntnerstrasse and the Graben are all within walking distance. Even the Kunsthistorisches Museum (Museum of Fine Arts) and Karlskirche are only just outside the Ringstrasse that marks the medieval precincts of the 1st District.

The best way to view the formidable monuments along the Ringstrasse is by tram (*Strassenbahn*; VRT, Vienna Ring Tram, runs around the Ring). Trams also cover some 30 routes to outlying districts and provide a good, cheap way of reaching other parts of the city on your trip, for instance Schönbrunn Palace or a *Heuriger* wine garden. The U-Bahn subway system has five lines, numbered U1 to U6 (U5 has not yet been built). U1 and U3 intersect in the city centre at Stephansplatz. The other most conveniently located station is Karlsplatz.

INNERE STADT

STEPHANSDOM

The imposing **Stephansdom** ❶ (St Stephen's Cathedral; Mon–Sat 6am–10pm, Sun 7am–10pm; free; www.stephanskirche. at), located right in the heart of Vienna, is the best place to start a tour. Whichever way you choose to walk through the Innere Stadt most inevitably gravitate towards the cathedral at some point. For more than eight centuries it has watched over Vienna, enduring city fires, Turkish cannonballs and German and Russian shells. Part of the Stephansdom's charm

Vienna viewed from the steeple of the Stephansdom

derives from the asymmetry of its steeple, set to one side. Affectionately known as *Steffl*, it is 137m (449ft) high. Count 343 steps to the **observation platform** at the top, where the view extends northeast to the Czech Republic and southwest to the Semmering Alps.

The main portal takes its name, **Riesentor** (Giant's Gate), from a huge bone found during construction in the 13th century, which was thought to be the shin of a giant drowned in Noah's flood. Scientists subsequently concluded it was the tibia of a mammoth.

With its Romanesque western facade, Gothic tower and baroque altars, the cathedral epitomises Vienna's genius for harmonious compromise, here managing seamlessly to meld the austerity, dignity and exuberance of three architectural styles. The Romanesque origins (1240) are strikingly visible in the breathtaking **Heidentürme** (Heathen Towers) and statuary depicting, among others, a griffin and Samson fighting a lion. Above the entrance are Jesus, the Apostles and a veritable menagerie of dragons, lions, reptiles and birds representing evil spirits to be exorcised by the sanctity of the church.

The mainly Gothic structure we see today was built in the 14th and 15th centuries. To support their petition to have Vienna made a bishopric, the Habsburgs hoped to impress the Pope by adding a second tower. But the city fathers preferred to spend the money on strengthening city fortifications against the Turks and Protestants, so the **North Tower** was never properly completed, just topped off in 1578 with a frivolous Renaissance cupola. From atop the tower (accessible by lift) a fine view of the city opens up. In the tower swings the 20-tonne **Pummerin bell**, a recast version of the one made from the bronze of Turkish cannons captured after the 1683 siege, but destroyed in the wartime fire of 1945. It is only rung on special occasions such as New Year's Eve.

Inside the church, in the centre aisle, is the wonderfully carved Gothic **pulpit** by Master Anton Pilgram (1455–1515). At the head of the spiral staircase the sculptor has placed the figures of Augustine, Gregory, Jerome and Ambrose, fathers of the Church – and added a sculpture of himself looking through a window under the staircase. No shrinking violet, Pilgram pops up again at the foot of the elaborate stone organ base he built in the north aisle.

Left of the high altar is the carved wooden **Wiener Neustädter Altar**. To the right is the marble **tomb** of Emperor

Sculptor Master Pilgram at the foot of the organ base

Stephansplatz and the Haas Haus

Friedrich III (died 1493), honoured by the Viennese for having the city made a bishopric and for inventing the *Semmel*, the little bread roll you receive with every meal.

Mass is held at 10.15am on Sunday and holidays (9.30am July and August). There are guided tours and roof walks, as well as tours of the bone-filled catacombs.

Opposite the Stephansdom looms the contrasting **Haas Haus**, a large, curved building whose windows reflect a distorted cathedral. This hinge between Graben and Stephansplatz was erected in 1990 to plans by Hans Hollein. Stephansplatz joins **Stock-im-Eisen-Platz** (literally meaning 'stick set in iron'), a name which refers to a gnarled old tree trunk on the corner of the Graben and Kärntnerstrasse into which journeymen locksmiths arriving in medieval Vienna would drive a nail for good luck. The nails are now protected by a Plexiglas shield.

EAST OF STEPHANSDOM

If you're looking for a place to unwind after visiting the cathedral, walk east along Rotenturmstrasse to one of the outdoor cafés on **Lugeck**, a pleasant little square where burglars used to be hanged some 300 years ago. Or wander further over to the **Fleischmarkt**, where, at No. 11, you'll discover Vienna's oldest tavern, the **Griechenbeisl** (1490), once frequented by the likes of Mozart, Beethoven, Schubert, Strauss and Mark Twain, as well as by Marx Augustin (see panel).

Around the corner on Grashofgasse, cross the pretty courtyard of the 17th-century **Heiligenkreuzerhof** abbey, one of the Innere Stadt's most attractive nooks, to the **Basiliskenhaus** (Schönlaterngasse 7), steeped in medieval superstition. Here a basilisk – half rooster, half lizard – was said to have lived in a well and breathed its poisonous fumes into the drinking water, until one day a baker's apprentice held up a mirror to the monster and scared it to death.

From here it's a Mozartkugel's throw to the **Alte Universität** (Old University, 1365), where young Franz Schubert lived as a member of the Vienna Boys' Choir. The Alte Universität was closed down after student demonstrations in 1848 against the autocratic regime of Metternich, and the hotheads were moved out of the Innere Stadt to academies in the outer districts until a new university was opened in 1884, safely on the outer edge of the Ring.

On Bäckerstrasse, the baroque house of the old Schmauswaberl restaurant (No. 16) served students with leftovers from the Hofburg kitchens. The French lady of letters Madame de Staël lived at the Palais Seilern, and across the street (at No. 7) is a beautiful ivy-covered arcaded Renaissance courtyard.

Cut across the busy Wollzeile to **Domgasse 5**, where, from 1784 to 1787, Wolfgang Amadeus Mozart lived. The house is now a museum, the **Mozarthaus Vienna** ❷ (daily 10am–7pm; U-Bahn 1, 3: Stephansplatz; www.mozart hausvienna.at), which was completely revamped and

Du lieber Augustin

This famous Viennese folk song tells the story of a local itinerant bagpiper – Marx Augustin – who, while drunk late at night, fell into a pit filled with the bodies of dead plague victims, and lived to tell the tale.

reopened in time for the 250th anniversary celebrations in 2006. Mozart wrote 11 piano concertos here, as well as one horn concerto, two quintets, four quartets, three trios, three piano sonatas, two violin sonatas and the opera *The Marriage of Figaro*. Just around the corner, in Rauhensteingasse, the composer struggled to finish the *Requiem* before his early death. His coffin was assigned to an anonymous grave in the St Marxer Friedhof.

Cheer up with a stroll through the **Fähnrichshof** at the corner of Blutgasse and Singerstrasse. This charming complex of artists' studios, galleries, boutiques, apartments and gardens is a triumph of urban renovation from the ruin left by World War II bombs. The nearby **Franziskanerplatz** presents a fine baroque ensemble – an 18th-century fountain with a statue of Moses by Johann Martin Fischer, the elegant **Franziskanerkirche** (Mon–Sat 7am–6pm) and the Kleines Café, tastefully remodelled by Hermann Czech.

Lobmeyr on Kärntnerstrasse

KÄRNTNERSTRASSE TO ALBERTINAPLATZ

Kärntnerstrasse was once the city's main north–south thoroughfare, continuing on through Carinthia (Kärnten) to Trieste on the Adriatic. It has always been the central artery of Viennese social life, perhaps because it joins the sacred and the cultural heart of Vienna – the Stephansdom at one end and the Staatsoper (Opera House) at the other.

The street, which has been transformed into a traffic-free pedestrian zone, is now a bit of a commercial disgrace, disfigured by oversize plastic illuminated signs. However, it still contains some of Vienna's historic shops. Most are modern, but the **Lobmeyr** shop (No. 26) dates back to 1823. The Gothic **Malteserkirche** (No. 37) was founded by the crusading Knights Hospitallers.

Just off Kärntnerstrasse, on Neuer Markt, is the **Kapuzinerkirche** (Church of the Capuchin Friars). Beneath it is the 17th-century imperial burial vault, the **Kaisergruft** (daily 10am–6pm; www.kaisergruft.at), also known as the Kapuzinergruft. Among the tombs and sarcophagi of some 140 Habsburgs, note the double casket of Maria Theresa and her husband, François de Lorraine. The most recent burial was in 1989, of Zita, wife of the last emperor, Karl I (who abdicated in 1918 and is buried in Madeira). Franz Joseph and Empress Elisabeth (Sissi) are apparently still much loved, their coffins festooned with flowers.

On Philharmonikerstrasse is the **Hotel Sacher ❸**, which opened in 1882. Anna Sacher, who presided over its early days, was a renowned hostess, anticipating her guests' every need. She attracted courtiers, aristocrats, diplomats and the rich, even embroidering their signatures on a tablecloth. The famous chocolate cake, the *Sachertorte*, is actually 50 years older than the hotel; it was created by Franz Sacher in 1832 for Prince Metternich when he wanted something new and impressive for an important occasion.

At the intersection of Kärntnerstrasse and the Ringstrasse stands the **Staatsoper ❹** (Opera House; guided tours usually at 1, 2 and 3pm; www.wiener-staatsoper.at).

The original Opera House, inaugurated in 1869, was greeted with such criticism that one of the architects, Edward van der Nüll, was driven to suicide. It was almost completely destroyed in the 1945 bombardments, but rebuilt to the original design.

A lot about the opera's orchestra, from which the Wiener Philharmoniker is derived, can be learnt at the nearby **Haus der Musik ❺** (Seilerstätter 30; daily 10am–10pm; U-Bahn 1, 3: Oper; tram 2, D, 71, VRT: Schwarzenberg Platz; www.hdm. at). Exhibitions are spread over three floors, of which the first has a display on the history of the Wiener Philharmoniker, with a 'compose your own waltz' game. Upstairs is the **Klangmuseum**, an exploration of sound with fun interactive exhibits. The third floor has displays on some of the most famous composers to have worked in Austria.

Just beside the Staatsoper is **Albertinaplatz**. On the far side of the square is the Lobkowicz Palace, now home to the **Österreichisches Theatermuseum** (Wed–Mon 10am–6pm; U-Bahn 1, 2, 4: Karlsplatz; U-Bahn 1, 3: Oper; tram 1, 2, 62, D, VRT: Oper; www.theatermuseum.at). Inside are models of theatres, costumes and set designs, as well as the beautifully decorated Eroica Saal where Beethoven's Third Symphony was first performed. The museum's collection was recently expanded to include the contents of the Staatsopernmusem, which closed in 2014.

Also on Albertinaplatz is the bleak **Monument against War and Fascism** (1991) by Alfred Hrdlicka. Facing the stone gate symbolising totalitarian force is the controversial bronze sculpture of a kneeling figure, recalling the humiliation of Jews forced by the Nazi regime to scrub pavements with a toothbrush.

Opposite the monument is the **Albertina ❻**, the Habsburg palace that contains the **Graphische Sammlung Albertina**

Bronze sculpture recalling Nazi oppression

(Albertinaplatz 1; daily 10am–6pm, Wed until 9pm; charge; www.albertina.at). Named after Maria Theresa's son-in-law, Duke Albert of Saxony-Teschen, and founded in 1781, this palace holds one of the world's finest collections of graphic art, with more than 60,000 original drawings and over a million wood and copperplate prints. The collection showcases major artists from the 15th century to the present day, including priceless works by Dürer, da Vinci, Michelangelo, Raphael, Titian, Rembrandt, Rubens, Van Gogh, Toulouse-Lautrec, Beardsley and Grosz.

The state rooms were restored a few years ago and an exhibition space created together with storage and retrieval facilities. Any of the drawings can be viewed by written request.

Just below the Albertina, with its entrance on Albertinaplatz, is Austria's **Filmmuseum** (Augustinerstrasse 1; Mon–Thur 10am–6pm, Fri until 1pm; www.filmmuseum.at), which puts on an exciting programme of art-house and period films, many taken from its comprehensive archive.

THE GRABEN AND THE JEWISH QUARTER

Running northwest from Stephansplatz, the Graben, together with the adjacent Kohlmarkt and Dorotheergasse, is the centre of Vienna's most fashionable shops and coffee houses. Until the demise of the Habsburgs, it was equally infamous for its Graben nymphs, as the local ladies of the night were known. The Graben and its extension, Naglergasse, mark the southern boundary of the original Roman settlement of Vindobona; the approximate square shape is completed by Rotenturmstrasse to the east, Salzgries to the north and Tiefer Graben to the west.

The Graben is now a pedestrian zone, dominated by the startling, bulbous-shaped monument to the town's deliverance from the plague in 1679. The **Pestsäule** (Plague Column) combines humility before God and gruesome fascination with the disease itself. A more joyous celebration of faith, just off the Graben, is the **Peterskirche ❼** (St Peter's Church; Mon–Fri 7am–8pm, Sat–Sun 9am–9pm), designed in 1702 by Gabriele Montani and completed by Johann Lukas von Hildebrandt. The exterior embraces the graceful oval of its nave, its rows of pews curving outwards, each decorated with three carved angels' heads. It displays the genius of Viennese baroque for marrying the sumptuous with the intimate.

The Plague Column on the Graben

South of Stephansplatz, at Dorotheergasse 11, is the **Jüdisches Museum ❽** (Jewish Museum; Sun–Fri 10am–6pm; U-Bahn 1, 3: Stephansplatz; www.jmw.at). The museum is housed in the 18th-century Palais Eskeles, formerly the property of a prominent Jewish financier.

The oval nave of the 18th-century Peterskirche

It traces the history of the city's Jewish community from the Middle Ages, through the years of its illustrious contributions to Viennese culture, to its extermination by German and Austrian Nazis in World War II. Temporary exhibitions are also staged here, usually devoted to prominent artists, writers and other historical figures of Viennese life. Despite the community's tragic end, the museum's approach is positive, reinforced by a cheery café and bookshop on the ground floor.

The old **Jewish Quarter**, still in large part a garment district, lies north of Stephansplatz and the Graben. Its medieval centre was **Judenplatz** (Jews' Square) until the pogrom of 1421, when the synagogue was dismantled and its stones carted off to build an extension to the Alte Universität. The remains of the synagogue have been excavated and now form part of the elaborate **Museum Judenplatz Wien** (Sun–Thur 10am–6pm, Fri 10am–2pm), which functions as an annexe to the Jüdisches Museum on Dorotheergasse. On the square is Rachel Whiteread's **Memorial to the Victims of the Holocaust**, which commemorates more than 65,000 Austrian Jews who were killed by the Nazis and is designed to resemble a library turned inside out, the shelves of closed books face inwards.

The one **synagogue** out of the city's 24 that survived the Nazis' 1938 *Kristallnacht* pogrom is at Seitenstettengasse 4, next to a kosher restaurant (guided tours Mon–Thur 11.30am and 2pm; a combined ticket for the museums allows you to view the synagogue free). With its Jewish community centre, it stands behind an apartment block beside the unusual **Kornhäuselturm** (1827), studio and home of architect Josef Kornhäusel. Inside is a drawbridge he pulled up whenever he wanted to shut himself off from his quarrelsome wife.

Around the corner is the city's oldest church, the ivy-covered Romanesque **Ruprechtskirche** (Wed and Sat 12.15–3.30pm, Thur–Fri 12.15–4pm), which is dedicated to Rupert, patron saint of salt – a valuable commodity in earlier times.

Memorial to the Victims of the Holocaust

From here, cut back through Judengasse to the **Hoher Markt**. This was once the forum of Roman Vindobona, and a small Römermuseum at No. 3 (Tue–Sun 9am–6pm; free entry on the first Sun of each month; www.wienmuseum.at) shows remains of two Roman houses laid bare by a 1945 bombardment. At the east end of the square is a gem of high Viennese kitsch, the **Ankeruhr**, an animated clock built in 1911 by an insurance company. Charlemagne, Prince Eugene, Maria Theresa, Joseph Haydn and others perform their act at midday.

At the western end of Hoher Markt, turn right into Marc Aurel-Strasse, named after the Roman emperor who died in AD 180. On the left, Salvatorgasse leads behind the **Altes Rathaus** (Old Town Hall), which now contains the **Archive of the Austrian Resistance** (Mon–Thur 9am–5pm; www.doew.at), and past the superb porch of the **Salvatorkapelle**, a happy marriage of Italian Renaissance and Austrian late Gothic sculpture. Beyond it is the slender 14th-century Gothic church of **Maria am Gestade** (Mary on the Banks), originally overlooking the Danube. Notice its delicate tower, the canopied porch, and remains of Gothic stained glass in the choir.

PLATZ AM HOF

Walk back across the Judenplatz to the spacious **Platz am Hof**, the largest square in the old part of the city. The Babenberg dukes, predecessors of the Habsburgs, built their fortress here in about 1150. It was both a military stronghold and a palace for festivities such as the grand state reception in 1165 for German emperor Friedrich Barbarossa. The **Mariensäule** (Virgin's Column) was erected in 1667 to celebrate victory over Sweden's armies in the Thirty Years War. It was on a lamppost in the middle of this square that the revolutionaries of 1848 hanged war minister Theodor Latour. The end of the Holy Roman Empire, said by some to be neither holy nor Roman nor an empire, was proclaimed with fanfare at the baroque **Am Hof** church in 1806.

Along the narrow street to the left of the church is the **Uhrenmuseum** (Clock Museum; Tue–Sun 10am–6pm; free entry on the first Sun of each month; www.wienmuseum.at). Set in one of the oldest buildings in Vienna, with an attractive spiral staircase, it has some interesting exhibits (if you are into timepieces), including the huge workings of the original Stephansdom clock (1699) and the 18th-century astronomical clock made by the German watchmaker David Cajetano.

AROUND HERRENGASSE

In Bognergasse, notice the pretty *Jugendstil* facade of the **Engel-Apotheke** (1907) before returning to medieval Vienna through narrow, cobbled Naglergasse. This leads to the **Freyung** triangle, flanked by the Palais Harrach dating from 1690 (where Joseph Haydn's mother was once the family cook; now a venue for temporary exhibitions mounted by the Kunsthistorisches Museum) and the **Schottenkirche** (Church of the Scots), founded by Scottish and Irish Benedictine monks in the 12th century, whose monastery has an excellent **picture gallery** (Tue–Fri 11am–5pm, Sat 11am–4.30pm; www.schottenstift.at).

Art forum

At Freyung 8, the Kunstforum der Bank Austria (Sat–Thur 10am–7pm, Fri 10am–9pm; www.bankaustria-kunstforum. at) mounts first-class exhibitions of contemporary art and sculpture, and paintings from the 19th and 20th centuries.

To the north of the Freyung, just before the Ringstrasse, Schottengasse leads to the Mölker Bastei and the **Pasqualatihaus** (Tue–Sun 10am–1pm, 2–6pm; free entry on the first Sun of each month; U-Bahn 2, 4, tram 1, 43, 44, D, VRT: Schottentor; www.wien museum.at). Beethoven lived in this house on several occasions between 1803 and 1815 at the invitation of his friend and patron, Baron Johann Baptist of Pasqualati. Here he composed parts of *Fidelio* and his Fourth to Seventh symphonies, as well as his Piano Concerto in G-major (Opus 58). Today it is one of three Beethoven residences in Vienna open to the public as museums (see also pages 73 and 75).

South of the Freyung is Herrengasse, the Innere Stadt's main eastbound traffic artery, lined with imposing baroque and neo-baroque

Relaxing in Café Central

palaces, now serving as government offices or embassies. Here, too, stands the 18th-century **Palais Ferstel**, incorporating an elegant shopping arcade, Freyung Passage, and the renovated **Café Central**, Vienna's leading coffee house before World War I (see page 108). Upstairs, a restaurant occupies the gilded premises of the old stock exchange.

Herrengasse leads to Michaelerplatz and the Hofburg. Once the imperial parish church, **Michaelerkirche** (Mon–Sat 7am–10pm, Sun and holidays 8am–10pm) is a hybrid mixture of Romanesque, Gothic and baroque. At No. 5 is the architecturally revolutionary **Looshaus**, now a bank. Built by Adolf Loos, its starkly functional use of fine materials shocked many in 1910. Emperor Franz Joseph so hated its 'outrageously naked' facade that he stopped using the Hofburg's Michaelertor exit.

Sissi, Vienna's famous princess

THE HOFBURG

Defeat in war took away the Habsburgs, but not the palaces. The most imposing is the **Hofburg** (Michaelerplatz 1; U-Bahn 2: Babenbergerstrasse or Herrengasse; tram 1, 2, D, VRT: Burgring), home of Austria's rulers since the 13th century.

Covering the southwest corner of the Innere Stadt, the vast palace went through five major stages of construction over six centuries, and at the end there was still a large unfinished section. Today, the palace's museums exhibit most of the vast personal fortune of the Habsburgs.

IMPERIAL APARTMENTS

To sense the human scale of the gigantic enterprise, start by taking the 45-minute guided tour of the **Kaiserappartements** (Imperial Apartments; daily Sept–June 9am–5.30pm, July–Aug 9am–6pm; www.hofburg-wien.at). Coming from the Michaelerplatz, the entrance is to the left of the Hofburg rotunda. You will see splendid Gobelins tapestries; a smoking room for the emperor's fellow officers; enormous rococo stoves needed to heat the place; a crystal chandelier weighing half a tonne; Franz Joseph's austere bedroom with iron military camp-bed; and rooms used by his wife, Elisabeth (Sissi), including her newly restored drawing room and bedroom, and the gymnasium she used for daily exercise, complete with wall bars and climbing ropes.

The first six rooms, the so-called Stephansappartement, are devoted to the **Sissi Museum**. This examines the life of the empress from her carefree childhood in Bavaria to her murder at the hands of an anarchist in Geneva. Particular emphasis is placed on the private life of Elisabeth, including her obsessive exercise regimes and fixation with beauty.

SILVER COLLECTION

To the right of the Hofburg rotunda coming from the Michaelerplatz is the **Hofsilber und Tafelkammer** (Imperial Silver and Tableware Collection; same times as the Imperial Apartments). On display are the priceless Chinese, Japanese,

THE LIFE AND DEATH OF AN EMPRESS

Elisabeth, affectionately known as Sissi, was a Bavarian princess and a legend both in her own lifetime and more than a century after her death. Married to Emperor Franz Joseph 1 in 1854 when she was just 16, she was never at home with the oppressive formality of court life, but her presence still made the court the most glittering in Europe. She was noted for her stringent exercise and beauty regime (she spent hours on her hair), and her hairdresser was a confidante who sometimes took her mistress's place during boring functions where the empress would not be closely scrutinised.

As she grew older, Sissi was able to lead her own life, travelling extensively which gave her a love for the imperial train. In 1898, at the age of 60, she was fatally stabbed by an Italian anarchist in Geneva. In Austria and Hungary she is still a figure of enchantment; a Winterhalter portrait of Sissi with stars in her hair, old romantic films and, most recently, a musical about her life have, perhaps, kept memories fresh.

A Lipizzaner performing at the Spanish Riding School

French Sèvres and German Meissen services amassed by the Habsburgs over six centuries of weddings and birthdays. Highlights include a 140-piece service in vermeil and a neo-Renaissance centrepiece given to Emperor Franz Joseph by Queen Victoria in 1851.

THE STALLBURG

In 1533, four years after the Turks were repulsed, Ferdinand I felt safe enough to settle in the Hofburg, bringing his barons and bureaucrats to make their homes in nearby Herrengasse and Wallnerstrasse. He built the **Stallburg** in 1565 (outside the main Hofburg complex on Reitschulgasse) as a home for his son Archduke Maximilian, subsequently turned into stables for the Spanish Riding School. With its fine three-storey arcaded courtyard, the Stallburg is the most important Renaissance building in Vienna. After an outbreak of infection some years ago the stables are no longer open to the public.

SPANISH RIDING SCHOOL

Part of the massive expansion of the Hofburg that took place in the 17th and 18th centuries is the magnificent parade hall of the **Winterreitschule**, home of the **Spanische Reitschule** ❿ (Spanish Riding School), right opposite the Stallburg. It is worth visiting on architectural grounds alone: constructed between 1729 and 1735, it is the work of Josef Emanuel Fischer von Erlach and is considered a masterpiece of the baroque era.

The Lipizzaner horses perform in its elegant arena throughout the year, except in July. Tickets must be booked well in advance (performances Sat and/or Sun 11am; guided tours daily; www.srs.at; performances can be booked in advance online, and the daily schedule is posted on leaflets outside the entrance under the Michaelertor). A cheaper option is to watch the horses train. Morning exercises are held between 10am and noon, usually Tuesday to Friday or Saturday except in July (tickets available on the day from 9am).

The Lipizzaners, originally a Spanish breed, were raised at Lipica in Slovenia, not far from Trieste; since 1920 the tradition has been carried on in the Styrian town of Piber. Using methods unchanged since the 17th century, the horses are trained to perform complex steps and dances.

The Great Hall of the National Library

NATIONAL LIBRARY

Beside the Spanish Riding School complex is **Josefsplatz**, a marvellously harmonious baroque square, in the middle of which stands Franz Anton Zauner's equestrian statue (1795–1807) of Emperor Joseph II.

Behind stands the main building of the **Österreichische Nationalbibliothek** (Austrian National Library), which contains more than

The Vienna Boys' Choir sings in the Schweizerhof

2 million manuscripts and printed books, as well as maps, portraits, musical scores, papyrus documents and a globe museum. The building – the former Imperial Library – is one of the most important works of the court architect Johann Bernhard Fischer von Erlach, but it was built between 1723 and 1735 under the supervision of his son, Josef Emanuel. The highlight is the **Prunksaal** (Great Hall; Fri–Wed 10am– 6pm, Thur 10am–9pm; www.onb.ac.at), one of the world's greatest secular baroque interiors. The ceiling frescoes (1730) by Daniel Gran depict the apotheosis of the library's founder, Emperor Charles VI.

The baroque **Augustinerkirche** was traditionally the Habsburgs' wedding church. It was here that Maria Theresa married François of Lorraine in 1736, Marie-Louise married Napoleon *(in absentia)* in 1810, and Franz Joseph married Elisabeth in 1854. Although the Habsburgs' burial church is the Kapuzinerkirche over on Neuer Markt, the heart of the deceased was buried deep in the Augustiner crypt.

SCHWEIZERHOF

The **Schweizerhof** (Swiss Court), the oldest part of the Hofburg, is named after the Swiss Guard once housed there. Here King Ottokar of Bohemia built a fortress in 1275 to resist Rudolf von Habsburg. Victorious Rudolf moved in and strengthened the fortifications to keep out the unruly Viennese. By the archway are the pulleys for the chains of the drawbridge. But Rudolf's son, Albrecht I, preferred the safety of Leopoldsberg in the Vienna Woods. For 250 years, the fortress was used only for ceremonial occasions. The **Burgkapelle** (Castle Chapel; Sept–June Mon–Tue 10am–2pm, Fri 11am–1pm; www.hofmusikkapelle.gv.at) was built in 1449. Originally Gothic, it was redone in baroque style and then partially restored to its original form in 1802.

In the Schweizerhof, the **Schatzkammer** ⑫ (Treasury; Thur 10am–9pm, June–Aug Fri–Wed 10am–6pm, Sept–May Tue–Wed and Fri–Sun 10am–6pm; www.khm.at) contains a dazzling display of the insignia of the old Holy Roman Empire. Highlights are the imperial crown of pure unalloyed gold set with pearls and unpolished emeralds, sapphires and rubies. First used in AD 962 for the coronation of Otto the Great in Rome, it moved on to Aachen and Frankfurt for crowning successors. Also

VIENNA BOYS' CHOIR

The Wiener Sängerknaben (Vienna Boys' Choir) was founded in 1498 as part of the Imperial Chapel choir with 16 to 20 choirboys. It increased steadily in size over the years, and in the 18th and 19th centuries included Josef Haydn and Franz Schubert among its members. Re-established in 1924, it today consists of four individual choirs, each having 24 members. The choir sings Mass on Sunday and at Church festivals in the Burgkapelle (www.wienersaengerknaben.at).

The imperial crown

on display are the sword of Charlemagne and the Holy Lance, which is said to have pierced the body of Christ on the Cross and which has been claimed by some, including Hitler, to have mystical powers. Other intriguing artefacts include a unicorn's horn and an agate bowl, reputed to be the Holy Grail used by Christ at the Last Supper.

IN DER BURG

The Schweizertor (Swiss Gate) leads into the busy square known as **In der Burg**, which is surrounded by buildings from various eras. Leopold I launched the city's baroque era with his **Leopoldinischer Trakt** (Leopoldine Wing) – a residence in keeping with the Habsburgs' role as a world power. Constructed in 1660–66 by Domenico and Martin Carlone, to a design by Philiberto Luchesi, it serves today as the official residence of the president of Austria.

The **Amalienburg**, which was started under Emperor Maximilian II in the early baroque style, was finished in 1611 during the reign of Emperor Rudolf II by Pietro Ferrabosco and Antonio de Moys. It was named after Amalia of Brunswick, the consort of Emperor Joseph I.

The **Reichskanzleitrakt** housed the imperial administration until 1806. It was designed by Johann Lukas von Hildebrandt and Josef Emanuel Fischer von Erlach between 1723 and 1730; the four sculptures *(The Labours of Hercules)* are the work of Lorenzo Mattielli, who was active at the same time.

NEUE BURG

A passage leads from In der Burg to spacious **Heldenplatz**
(Heroes' Square). At the end of the 19th century, Franz Joseph
embarked on building a gigantic Kaiser Forum. This was to
have embraced the vast Heldenplatz with two crescent-shaped
arms, the whole extending through triumphal arches to the
Naturhistorisches and Kunsthistorisches museums. Only the
first of the two crescents, the **Neue Burg**, was built before the
empire collapsed. Today, it houses a congress centre, several
museums, and reading rooms for the National Library.

The building contains perhaps the most Viennese of all collections in the Hofburg, the
exquisite **Sammlung alter**
Musikinstrumente (Period
Musical Instruments Collection; Wed–Sun 10am–6pm;
www.khm.at), comprising
some 360 pieces, including
Renaissance instruments
representing practically everything blown, strummed
or tinkled up to the 17th
century. Also on display
are Haydn's harpsichord,
Beethoven's piano of 1803
and an 1839 piano used by
Schumann and Brahms.

The other museums in the
Neue Berg are the **Hofjagd**
und Rüstkammer (Collection
of Arms and Armour; Wed–
Sun 10am–6pm; www.khm.
at) and the **Ephesos Museum**

Statue of Eugene of Savoy
on Heldenplatz

Statue of Mozart in the Burggarten

(same times), with exhibits from excavations at the site in Turkey. The star attraction when it fully reopens after a lengthy renovation will be the **Museum für Völkerkunde** (closed for renovation until autumn of 2017; www.ethnomuseum.ac.at), the ethnographic collections of the Habsburgs.

THE BURGGARTEN

The **Burggarten**, the Hofburg's park, was laid out for the imperial family in the early 19th century. It has monuments to Franz Joseph I (1908, by Klimbusch) and Mozart (1896, by Viktor Tilgner), the latter moved here from Albertinaplatz in 1953. There is also the early 20th-century *Jugendstil* Palmenhaus (Glass House) by Friedrich Ohmann. This contains a lovely café, and the Schmetterlinghaus, a butterfly garden (Apr–Oct Mon–Fri 10am–4.45pm, Sat–Sun 10am–6.15pm, Nov–Mar daily 10am–3.45pm; www.schmetterlinghaus.at).

RINGSTRASSE AND ITS MUSEUMS

After the Hofburg, take a walk (or tram ride) around the Ringstrasse, the single urban achievement of Franz Joseph I. This boulevard, encircling the Innere Stadt, was created in the 1860s along the route of the old city walls.

Start west of the Schottenring, at the **Votivkirche** (Tue–Fri 2–6pm, Sat 9am–1pm and 4–6pm, Sun 9am–1pm), a neo-Gothic church built after Franz Joseph survived an assassination attempt in 1853. Next to it are the university and **Rathaus** (Town

Hall). Proceed along Universitätsring, and on the Innere Stadt side is the imposing **Burgtheater**, a high temple of German theatre. Beyond is the lovely **Volksgarten**, with its small buildings and scaled-down copy of the Athenian Temple of Theseus. Its cafés and concerts carry on a tradition that began with the café music of the Strauss family.

Opposite rises the temple-like **Parlament**, built by Theophil Hansen after a long sojourn in Athens. The ring then curves round to become the Burg Ring, flanked on the Innere Stadt side by the Hofburg and on the other side by **Maria-Theresien-Platz**, which lies between the Kunsthistorisches Museum and Naturhistorisches Museum.

KUNSTHISTORISCHES MUSEUM

If the **Kunsthistorisches Museum** ⑭ (Museum of Fine Arts; Thur 10am–9pm, June–Aug Fri–Wed 10am–6pm, Sept–May Tue–Wed,

Maria-Theresien-Platz and the Kunsthistorisches Museum

Inside the Kunsthistorisches Museum

Fri–Sun 10am–6pm; U-Bahn 2: Babenbergerstrasse; tram 1, 2, D, VRT: Burgring; wheelchair access Burgring 5; www.khm.at) is less well known than the Louvre or the Prado, it may just be that the name is something of a mouthful. The collection, celebrating its 125th anniversary in 2016, is, quite simply, magnificent. Benefitting from the cultural diversity of the Habsburg Empire, it in fact encompasses a much broader spectrum of Western European art than many of its better-known counterparts. The **Gemäldegalerie** (Gallery of Paintings) on the first floor displays a dazzling array of European art from the 16th to 18th centuries. Dutch, Flemish, German and English works are in the east wing, left of the main entrance, and Italian, Spanish and French works in the west wing, to the right. You can't fail to be awestruck: there are masterpieces by Caravaggio, Dürer, Raphael, Rembrandt, Rubens, Titian, Velázquez, Vermeer, and an entire room devoted to Pieter Brueghel.

The lower floor contains an impressive, and beautifully displayed, collection of ancient Egyptian, Greek and Roman art, as well as the **Sculpture and Applied Arts Collection**, where the prized possession is Benvenuto Cellini's famous gold-enamelled **salt cellar** made for King François I of France. A highlight of the **Classical Antiquities Collection** is the exquisite **Gemma Augustea**, a 1st-century AD onyx cameo. The **Egyptian/Oriental Collection** contains, among other treasures, the burial chamber of Prince Kaninisut.

NATURHISTORISCHES MUSEUM

The architectural twin of the Kunsthistorisches Museum stands opposite: the **Naturhistorisches Museum** (Natural History Museum; Thur–Mon 9am–6.30pm, Wed 9am–9pm; U-Bahn 2, 3: Volkstheater; tram 1, 2, D, VRT: Dr Karl-Renner-Ring; www.nhm-wien.ac.at). The museum contains exhibits ranging from insects to dinosaurs, and an impressive collection of meteorites. The vast reserves derive in part from the private collections of François of Lorraine (1708–65), husband of Maria Theresa. Highlights include the 25,000-year-old figurine *The Venus of Willendorf*, a 117kg (260lb) giant topaz, and Maria Theresa's exquisite jewel bouquet made of precious stones.

MUSEUMSQUARTIER

Relaxing outside MUMOK

At the other side of Museumstrasse is the modern museum complex, the **MuseumsQuartier ⑮** (Visitor and Ticket Centre, Museumsplatz, daily 10am–7pm; U-Bahn 2, 3: Volkstheater; www.mqw.at). Comprising Fischer von Erlach's 18th-century former Hofstallungen (Imperial Stables) alongside stunning new buildings, it is home to **MUMOK** (Museum of Modern Art, Mon 2–7pm, Tue–Wed, Fri–Sun 10am–7pm, Thur 10am–9pm; www.mumok.at), with its fine collection of 20th-century work by artists such as Kandinsky,

Magritte and Warhol; the superb **Leopold Museum** (Wed–Mon 10am–6pm, Thur 10am–9pm; www.leopoldmuseum.org), featuring a wide selection of Austrian art dating from the 19th and 20th centuries and including works by Klimt, Schiele and Max Oppenheimer; and the **Architekturzentrum Wien** (Vienna Architecture Centre; daily 10am–7pm; www.azw.at), which, aside from a great café, hosts inspiring temporary shows. Contemporary art exhibitions can be viewed at the **Kunsthalle Wien** (Fri–Wed 11am–7pm, Thur 11am–9pm; www.kunsthalle wien.at). The **Tanzquartier** (Mon–Fri 9am–8pm, Sat 10am–8pm; www.tqw.at) is one of Europe's most important contemporary dance centres with performances, workshops, lessons and other dance-related events taking place from September through to June.

JUGENDSTIL

In Austria, *Jugendstil* (Art Nouveau) caught the imagination of the art world, and the result was the foundation of the Secession Movement by a group of renegade artists from the Academy in 1897. The central figure of the Secession was Gustav Klimt (1862–1918), whose erotic, fairytale-like painting and themes came to embody *Jugendstil*. One of the key tenets for artists such as Klimt and Koloman Moser, and the leading *Jugendstil* architects Otto Wagner and Josef Hoffmann, was the linking of function and aesthetic.

Klimt's decorative elegance was a particular source of inspiration for Egon Schiele (1890–1918), whose linearity and subtlety reveals the strong influence of the *Jugendstil*. Schiele, however, emphasised expression over decoration, concentrating on the human figure with an acute eroticism that was less decorative than Klimt's. Evocation of intense feeling through colours and lines was of equal importance to Oskar Kokoschka (1886–1980), a leading exponent of Expressionism.

FINE ARTS ACADEMY

The Ringstrasse gradually bends round to become the Opern Ring. On the right is Schillerplatz, home to the **Akademie der Bildenden Künste** (Academy of Fine Arts; Tue–Sun 10am–6pm; U-Bahn 1, 2, 4: Karlsplatz/Oper; tram 1, 2, D, VRT: Burgring; www.akademiegalerie. at). Few art academies can rival its outstanding collection of European paintings

The Secession Building

– particularly Dutch and Flemish masters – from the 14th century to the present day. Highlights include *The Last Judgement* by Hieronymus Bosch and works by Rubens, Rembrandt, Van Dyck, Pieter de Hooch and Tiepolo. The building itself was constructed in the 1870s to an Italian Renaissance design by Theophil Hansen.

SECESSIONSGEBÄUDE

Standing defiantly opposite, on the corner of Friedrichstrasse, is the distinctive **Secessionsgebäude** ⑯ (Secession Building; Tue–Sun 10am–6pm; U-Bahn 1, 2, 4: Karlsplatz; tram 1, 2, D, VRT: Burgring; www.secession.at). This is the gallery of the Secession Movement, which was formed when 19 artists (the most celebrated being Gustav Klimt) broke from what they saw as the reactionary Viennese art establishment in 1897. It was built by Josef Maria Olbrich, a student of Otto Wagner. An inscription above the door proclaims: *'Der Zeit ihre Kunst, der Kunst ihre Freiheit'* ('To the Age, its own Art; to Art, its own Freedom'). The building is topped with a golden dome of laurel leaves, known

Stadtbahn Pavilion by Secession architect Otto Wagner

locally as the 'golden cabbage', and said to symbolise the interdependence of art and nature. Contemporary work is also on show. In the basement is Klimt's large Beethoven Frieze, created for a Secession exhibition in 1902.

KARLSPLATZ

There are a number of attractions on and around nearby **Karlsplatz 17**. The elegant glass cube on Treitlstrasse is the **Kunsthalle Project Space** (Fri–Wed 11am–7pm, Thur until 9pm; U-Bahn 1, 2, 4: Karlsplatz; www.kunsthallewien.at), a branch of the Kunsthalle Wien (in the MuseumsQuartier), which stages exhibitions featuring topical themes and current trends in contemporary art. The café, with its giant terrace, is a favourite meeting place come night-time.

The square is dominated by the huge **Karlskirche** (Mon–Sat 9am–6pm, Sun noon–7pm; www.karlskirche.at), the most important of the city's baroque churches. It was built by Fischer von Erlach for Karl VI, fulfilling an oath made by the emperor during the plague of 1713. Sunset offers a spectacular view of the big dome across Karlsplatz. The cool, sober interior has a subdued marble decor and spacious oval ground plan similar to that of the Peterskirche. The oval dome's ceiling **frescoes** are by Johann Michael Rottmayr, the *trompe-l'oeil* by Gaetano Fanti. Notice, too, Daniel Gran's lovely painting of **St Elisabeth** in the main chapel on the right. In front of the church, Henry Moore's sculpture *Hill Arches* provides a striking contrast.

At the eastern end of Karlsplatz is **Wien Museum Karlsplatz**

(Tue–Sun 10am–6pm; free entry on the first Sun of each month; U-Bahn 1, 2, 4: Karlsplatz; www.wienmuseum.at). Displays cover the major historical events in the city, from the siege of 1529 to *fin de siècle* artistic movements, including a re-creation of the living room of architect Adolf Loos. There are fascinating models of the city before and after the development of the Ringstrasse.

Opposite is the magnificent neoclassical building of the **Musikverein** (Society of the Friends of Music; check website for guided tour dates and times; www.musikverein.at). Constructed in 1867 to a design by Theophil Hansen, it is home to the world-famous Vienna Philharmonic Orchestra. The ceiling paintings, *Apollo and the Nine Muses* (1911), are by August Eisenmenger.

The Musikverein

Beside the Musikverein lies the **Künstlerhaus** (1868), which houses art exhibitions (Fri–Sun, Tue–Wed 10am–6pm, Thur until 9pm; www.k-haus.at). In front are Otto Wagner's **Stadtbahn Pavilions** (Municipal Railway Pavilions), with their graceful green, gold and white motifs of sunflowers and tulips. Across the Kärntner Ring, the road becomes the Schubert and then the Park Ring as it barrels past the **Stadtpark**, home to the famous gilded bronze and marble monument to Johann Strauss the Younger.

APPLIED ARTS MUSEUM

On the same side of the Ring, across Weiskirchnerstrasse is the **Museum für Angewandte Kunst** ⑱ (Museum for Applied Arts; Wed–Sun 10am–6pm, Tue 10am–10pm, Tue 6–10pm; free; U-Bahn 3, tram 2, VRT: Stubentor; U-Bahn 4: Landstrasse; www.mak.at). Known simply as MAK, this is one of the city's most exciting and thought-provoking museums. The exhibition spaces are designed by contemporary artists who often reveal unexpected sides to quite mundane objects, such as the shadow play on Michael Thonet's bentwood chairs; you'll never view dining chairs in quite the same way again. There's a chance to see some particularly fine Viennese Biedermeier furnishings, as well as a collection of East Asian and Islamic art. The unmissable museum shop has a selection of items

BIEDERMEIER

The architecture, furniture and interior decoration known as 'Biedermeier' was produced in the period following Napoleon's defeat, between the Congress of Vienna in 1815 and the revolution in 1848. It was a time of political suppression in which the middle classes turned their attention to the arts. Biedermeier began as a satire, poking fun at the plodding German middle class. Two authors, Ludwig Eichrodt and Adolf Kussmaul, wrote poems in a journal called *Fliegende Blatter*, purporting to be the works of the unsophisticated 'Biedermeier', who, with his chum 'Bummelmeier', were boringly conventional. The name became synonymous with the age, but the work produced was far from dull. The Villa Wertheimstein (see page 73) and Dreimäderlhaus (Schreyvogelgasse 10) have fine examples of Biedermeier design; furniture is on display in the Museum for Applied Arts; and original pieces can still be found in antiques shops throughout the city, though they come with a hefty price tag.

– design-conscious, arty and some downright humorous.

Opposite the museum lies Dr Karl Lueger-Platz with its memorial to Dr Karl Lueger, the populist – and anti-Semitic – mayor of Vienna (1897–1910). The neighbouring **Café Prückel** is a welcome sight if you need a break. The Stubenring passes near the **Postsparkasse** (Savings Bank), another masterpiece by Otto Wagner.

OUTSIDE THE RING

The Innere Stadt and the Ringstrasse by no means have a monopoly on Vienna's

Hundertwasser Haus facade

sights. There's plenty more to be seen outside the Ring, from royal palaces to the Funeral Museum.

HUNDERTWASSER HAUS

Dismissed by many as a bit of a joke, the whimsical **Hundertwasser Haus ❿** is a hugely popular tourist attraction. This public housing complex in Kegelgasse was designed by Austria's best-known artist of recent times, Friedensreich Hundertwasser (1928–2000). The gently undulating facades of 52 apartments are decorated with bright paintwork, tiles, ceramics and onion domes. In the nearby Untere Weissgerberstrasse is Hundertwasser's own museum, the **Kunsthaus Wien** (daily 10am–6pm; tram 1, O: Radetzkyplatz; wheelchair access; www.kunsthauswien.com), which show both his work and

> ### Incineration plant
>
> Another of Friedensreich Hundertwasser's projects can be seen at the Fernwärmewerk at Spittelau (U-Bahn: Spittelau), an incinerator whose output is used to heat 60,000 homes. Decorated by the artist in a characteristically colourful way, it is crowned by a vast image of the artist's cap.

changing exhibitions by his contemporaries.

BELVEDERE

The summer palace of Prince Eugene of Savoy is regarded as the finest flower of Vienna's baroque residential architecture. Though close to the Innere Stadt, in the 3rd District, the **Belvedere** ⑳ (Unteres Belvedere, daily 10am–6pm; Oberes Belvedere, Thur–Tue 10am–6pm, Wed until 9pm; tram D; www.belvedere.at) is an enchanted world apart with its allegorical sculptures, fountains, waterfalls and gardens.

The **Unteres** (Lower) **Belvedere** was built by Johann Lukas von Hildebrandt in 1714–16, and served as Prince Eugene's summer residence. (His winter palace is another architectural gem, now brightening the lives of bureaucrats in the Finance Ministry on Himmelpfortgasse.) The palace was acquired by Maria Theresa after the prince's death, and was used by various members of the Habsburg dynasty, including Archduke Franz Ferdinand, whose assassination at Sarajevo in 1914 sparked off World War I. In 1955, the four victorious powers of World War II met in the Upper Belvedere to sign the treaty which confirmed Austria's independence as a neutral country.

The Lower Belvedere previously provided a home for the collection of baroque art, but this has now moved to the Oberes Belvedere and the space left is used for temporary exhibitions. Of the palace's exquisitely ornate interior the highlight is probably the highly adorned rococo gilt-and-mirrored Golden Cabinet. The palace's **Orangerie** (access through the Lower Belvedere) was previously the Museum of Medieval Art, but the permanent collection has for the most part, like the baroque works, moved to the Oberes Belvedere. The Orangerie is now used to share the exhibitions put on in the rest of the palace. Beside the Orangerie is the **Prunkstall** (10am–noon), part of the stables and now used to display some more of the extensive holdings of medieval art previously hidden in the museum's store rooms.

Prince Eugene held banquets and other festivities in the **Oberes** (Upper) **Belvedere**, completed in 1723. Today it houses a wide-ranging **collection** of Austrian art from the Middle Ages to the present day. The gallery reflects the Austro-Hungarian Empire's image as a declining world power, culminating in a final grand artistic fling around 1900. As well as the excellent collections of medieval and baroque art (the latter including works by Franz Anton Maulbertsch and Martino Altomonte),

Prince Eugene's summer palace, the Lower Belvedere (1716)

there are fine examples of German Romanticism (including works by Caspar David Friedrich). However, the star exhibits for most people are from the collections of the *fin de siècle* and the Vienna Secession. These include such masterpieces as *The Kiss* by Gustav Klimt and Egon Schiele and Oskar Kokoschka are also well represented. However, Klimt's portrait of *Adele Bloch-Bauer* no longer hangs in the gallery, as it was handed back to the Jewish family it had belonged to before the war (it was appropriated by the Nazis and had ended up in the Belvedere collection). The small but stunning collection of Impressionist and post-Impressionist art features works by Monet, Renoir, Cézanne, Van Gogh and Munch, and sculptures by Rodin and Degas.

The Kiss by Gustav Klimt

The Upper Belvedere **terrace** offers a splendid view of the city skyline, remarkably little changed since Bellotto-Canaletto painted it in 1760. For your walk through the gardens, the best place to start is at the Oberes Belvedere. The sunset view is a pure delight.

NEARBY MUSEUM

Close by in the Arsenal is the **Heeresgeschichtliches Museum** ㉑ (Museum of Military History, daily 9am–5pm; www.hgm.or.at). Housed in the earliest purpose-built museum in the city, the beautifully displayed, and extensive, holdings of the museum give a fascinating insight into the history of the Austrian state. The displays on World War II are hard-hitting, particularly the news footage of Vienna. One interesting, if slightly morbid, item on display is the blood-stained tunic of Archduke Franz Ferdinand which can be found next to the car in which he was assassinated.

ZENTRALFRIEDHOF

The Viennese, it must be said, do not consider it morbid to be interested in funerals and admire *eine schöne Leich* (a nice corpse). They enjoy a walk through the **Zentralfriedhof** (Central Cemetery; Simmeringer Hauptstrasse 234; daily Nov–Feb 8am–5pm, Mar, Oct 7am–6pm, Apr, Sept 7am–7pm, May–Aug 7am–8pm; tram 6, 71) in the southern district of Simmering. Opened in 1874, the cemetery has 200 hectares (500 acres) of funerary monuments that pay homage to the city's greats: musicians such as Beethoven, Schubert, Brahms and Schönberg, and writers Arthur Schnitzel and Franz Werfel. A map of the cemetery is available at Tor (Gate) 2.

The cemetery boasts the morbidly unique **Bestattungsmuseum** (Funeral Museum; Mon–Fri 9am–4.30pm, Mar–Oct also Sat 10am–5.30pm; tram 6, 71; www.bestattungsmuseum.at). At this typically Viennese institution you can find out about all sorts of curious items, including reusable coffins (after the ceremony, the hinged flaps would open, leaving the corpse behind while the coffin was taken off to be used again). The museum's ashtrays are inscribed *'Rauchen sichert Arbeitsplätze'* ('Smoking Guarantees Jobs').

THE GASOMETERS

Also in Simmering are the **Gasometers** (U-Bahn 3: Gasometer; www.wiener-gasometer.at). These four gasholders were built for the city in 1896–9. Following their decommissioning

One of the city's gasometers

in 1986, a scheme was launched to give the gasometers a new lease of life. Today the complex features shops, restaurants, cafés and bars, a multi-screen cinema and a hall seating 4,200 people. It's also home to offices, flats, student accommodation and the Vienna National Archives.

FURTHER SIGHTS

To the west of the Ringstrasse, leading out from the MuseumsQuartier (see page 53), is **Mariahilferstrasse**, the city's most popular shopping thoroughfare. Also, at No. 212, stands the **Technisches Museum** (Technical Museum; Mon–Fri 9am–6pm, Sat–Sun 10am–6pm; tram 52, 58: Penzinger Strasse; www.technischesmuseum.at). The main hall has steam engines, a huge steel-making crucible while aeroplanes swoop down from above. There are wheels to turn and levers to pull, making this a boredom-beating place for children, and the clearly laid-out exhibits explain the science behind many of the machines in an exemplary fashion.

Just to the south, along the Linke Wienzeile, are the fruit, vegetable and meat stalls of the famous **Naschmarkt** ㉒ (food market), which has been here since the 16th century. Originally it was beside a river, the Wienfluss. In the 19th century the river was roofed over and stalls set up on the roof. Notice the decorated Jugendstil facade of **Majolikahaus** at No.

40, by Secessionist architect Otto Wagner. Nearby is the venerable **Theater an der Wien**, built in 1801 for the impresario Emanuel Schikaneder, the librettist of Mozart's *Magic Flute*.

Further west is the **Haydnhaus** (Haydngasse 19; Tue–Sun 10am–1pm, 2pm–6pm; free entry on the first Sun of each month; U-Bahn 3: Zieglergasse; www.wienmuseum.at) where the composer lived from 1797 until his death on 31 May 1809. His two oratorios *The Creation* and *The Seasons* were conceived and written in this house.

Further west still, in the suburb of Penzing (14th District), is one of Otto Wagner's most important works, the **Kirche am Steinhof** (guided tour only, Sat 3pm; U-Bahn 4 to Unter St Veit then bus 47A). This masterpiece of *Jugendstil* design is the church for the Vienna's enlightened psychiatric hospital.

North of the Innere Stadt, at Berggasse 19, is the **Freud Museum** ㉓ (daily 10am–6pm; tram D: Schlickgasse; www.freud-museum.at), dedicated to the father of psychoanalysis. Sigmund Freud lived here from 1891 until the arrival of the Nazis in 1938, when he fled to England. While most of his books and belongings are in London (including the couch), the waiting room has been faithfully reconstructed, with advice from his daughter Anna Freud. The entrance hall is particularly evocative, with his hat, walking stick and suitcase initialled SF. The rooms where he did his consulting now have a display on his life, while the rest of the apartment is given over to temporary exhibitions. One fascinating room runs home movie footage showing Freud during his final years.

The elaborate Majolikahaus

Beyond the Freud Museum is the **Liechtenstein Museum** (the collection can only be viewed as part of guided tours held twice a month and pre-booked events, check the website for details; tram D: Bauernfeldplatz; www.liechtensteinmuseum.at), the garden palace of the princes of Liechtenstein. Now beautifully restored and showing off its wonderful frescoes, it holds an exceptionally fine collection of baroque paintings.

The **Schubert Geburtshaus** at Nussdorferstrasse 54 (Tue–Sun 10am–1pm, 2j–6pm; free entry on the first Sun of each month; tram 37, 38: Canisiusgasse; www.wienmuseum.at) is a museum set in the house where the composer was born in 1797.

SCHÖNBRUNN

Affairs of the state were not something Maria Theresa shied away from, but she did prefer to handle them in the calmer setting of **Schönbrunn** ㉔ (daily Nov–Mar 8.30am–5pm, Apr–June,

Schönbrunn in summer

Sept– Oct 8.30am–5.30pm, July–Aug 8.30am–6.30pm; U-Bahn 4: Schönbrunn; tram 10, 58: Schönbrunn; bus 10A: Schönbrunn; www.schoenbrunn.at). Almost as soon as she came to the throne in 1740, she moved into the palace, which Leopold I built as a summer residence and her father, Karl VI, had used as a shooting lodge. If the Hofburg is the oversized expression of a dynasty that outgrew itself, Schönbrunn is the

Schönbrunn garden walkway

smiling, serene expression of the personality of one woman, imperial nonetheless. Finding Fischer von Erlach's ideas for designing a 'super Versailles' too pompous, Maria Theresa brought in her favourite architect, Nikolaus Pacassi. He made Schönbrunn an imposing edifice, creating warm and decorative rococo interiors, which were a symbol of Maria Theresa's 'idyllic absolutism'.

THE GARDENS

To appreciate Schönbrunn's tendency to pleasure rather than imperial pomp, visit the **gardens** first. With the exception of the Kammergarten (Chamber Garden) and Kronprinzengarten (Crown Prince Garden) immediately left and right of the palace, the park has always been open to the public as Maria Theresa seems to have liked having the Viennese people around her. The park, laid out in classical French manner, is dominated by the **Gloriette,** a magnificent colonnade perched on the crest of a hill. It is difficult to say which view is prettier – the graceful

Sculpture at Schönbrunn

silhouette of the Gloriette against a sunset viewed from the palace, or a bright morning view from the Gloriette over the whole of Vienna to the north and the Wienerwald away to the south.

On the way to the Gloriette you will pass the Neptune Fountain and countless other statues of ancient mythology. East of the fountain are the half-buried artificial '**Roman ruins**', a romantic folly built by JF Hetzendorf von Hohenberg in 1778, complete with fragmented Corinthian columns, friezes and archways. Nearby is the Schöner Brunnen, the 'beautiful spring' discovered by Emperor Matthias around 1615, from which the palace took its name and which provided the water supply. West of Neptune is the **Tiergarten** (zoo), established in 1752 by François of Lorraine, the consort of Maria Theresa. Not everyone enjoys seeing animals behind bars, but the aquarium, with its 'walk-through' flooded rainforest, is worth a visit. You can also lose yourself in the topiary **maze** and a **Tyrolean Garden**. Other attractions include the **Palmenhaus** (Palm House) and **Wüstenhaus** (Desert Experience House).

THE PALACE

Crossing the courtyard to the palace's front entrance, you'll see on the right the **Schlosstheater**, now the site of summer chamber-opera performances.

A guided tour of the **palace** reveals something of the cosy ambience enjoyed by Maria Theresa and her successors: her breakfast room, decorated with the needlework of the empress and her myriad daughters; the **Spiegelsaal** (Hall of Mirrors), in which the young Mozart gave his first royal recital; the **Chinesisches Rundkabinett** (Chinese Round Room), also known as Maria Theresa's Konspirationstafelstube ('Top Secret Dining Room'). For her secret consultations, a table rose from the floor with a completely prepared dinner so that no servants would be present during the conversation. Guests used the **billiard room** while awaiting an audience with Franz Joseph. He, too, preferred Schönbrunn to the Hofburg and kept his mistress, actress Katharina Schratt, in a villa in the neighbouring district of Hietzing. Also on view is the bedroom where he died on 30 November 1916, at the age of 86.

The stately and the human are poignantly juxtaposed in the opulence of the ballrooms and dining rooms and the intimacy of the living quarters. The **Napoleon Room** (originally Maria Theresa's bedroom) was used by the French emperor on his way to victory at Austerlitz and by his son, the Duke of Reichstadt, in his final sad years. It is both pathetic and awesome to sense Napoleon's presence in a room that now contains his son's death mask and stuffed pet bird. Down the corridor, the last Habsburg (Karl I) abdicated at the end of World War I and Kennedy and Khrushchev

Flash fittings

The most ornate room at Schönbrunn is known as the Millions Room, with walls panelled in costly rosewood in the rococo style. Gilt-edged cartouches set into wood contain Indian miniature paintings showing the court and private lives of the 16th- and 17th-century Moghul emperors. To make them fit, original paintings were cut up by members of the imperial family and arranged as collages to form new pictures.

met for dinner at the height of the Cold War. In the adjoining **Wagenburg Museum** (May–Oct daily 9am–6pm, Nov–Apr 10am–4pm; www.khm.at) you can see an impressive collection of coaches used by the imperial court, including the gilded coronation carriage of Holy Roman Emperor Karl VI.

ACROSS THE DANUBE

THE PRATER

Over the Aspernbrücke, cross the Donaukanal at the junction of Franz-Josefs-Kai and Stubenring to reach the island between the Donaukanal and the much wider main channel to the east. The southern part is occupied by the **Prater** 🄯 (15 Mar–31 Oct daily 10am–midnight; free; www.praterservice. at). This is Vienna's most extensive park, once reserved for the nobility but opened up to the public in 1766 by Emperor Joseph II. In 2016 the Prater celebrated its 250th anniversary. Its most prominent feature is the old-fashioned amusement park with the famous **Riesenrad** 🄰 (Ferris Wheel; usually open all day long, see website for exact opening times; www.wienerriesenrad.com) that was immortalised in the

The Riesenrad at the Prater

film *The Third Man*. Built in 1897, it is one of the oldest and largest Ferris wheels in the world, 65m (213ft) high, and provides sweeping views over the city. Next to the Riesenrad is the terminal of the **Liliput-Bahn** (Lilliput Railway; www.liliputbahn. com), which provides transport around the park from mid-March to mid-October.

DONAUINSEL

You can reach the real Danube River (as opposed to the Danube Canal) along Lassallestrasse and over the Reichsbrücke. An artificial recreation island featuring beaches, barbecue picnic areas and sports facilities, the **Donauinsel** ❷ runs 21km (13 miles) along the middle of the river. The 'Blue Danube' is actually yellowish-brown in colour due to the lime content of the riverbed. Continue on the Wagramerstrasse, past the attractive modern complex of buildings forming the

The soaring Millennium Tower

UNO-City ❷ (officially the Vienna International Centre; guided tours Mon–Fri 11am, 2pm, 3.30pm; bring your passport; www.unvienna.org) to the **Alte Donau** (the Old Danube). This self-contained arm of the river is closed off for sailing, fishing and bathing, and is actually blue. The banks are lined with beaches, marinas and well-pruned gardens.

The **Donaupark** links the old and new Danube; more tranquil than the Prater, it has been laid out with flowerbeds, an artificial lake and sports arenas. It also features the 252m (827ft) tall **Donauturm** (Danube Tower), with fine views from its terrace. Back on the city side of the Danube, at Handelskai near the Nordbahnbrücke, is the **Millennium Tower** ❷. At over 200m (656ft), this is the tallest enclosed building in Central Europe.

Vienna viewed from the vineyards of Kahlenberg

VIENNA'S SUBURBS

You should devote at least a day to exploring the 19th District of **Döbling**, the most gracious and elegant of Vienna's suburbs. Stretching from the Danube Canal to the slopes of the Wienerwald, Döbling includes Sievering, Grinzing, Heiligenstadt, Nussdorf and Kahlenberg. It is dotted with villas, parks, vineyards and, of course, the *Heuriger* wine gardens, which are especially popular in **Grinzing**.

Heiligenstadt and the other neighbourhoods of Döbling provide a vital clue to the secret of Vienna's charm. Vienna is not a conventional big city, but rather a collection of villages clustered around the Innere Stadt. These village-suburbs provide a convenient getaway from what the Viennese call the *Hektik* of metropolitan life.

Catch tram D in front of the Votivkirche at Schottentor (or take U-Bahn 4 to its terminus), and take it to **Heiligenstadt**, the heart of Vienna's 'Beethoven country'. Call ahead to gain access to the **Eroica Haus** (Döblinger Hauptstrasse

92; by appointment only, call 01-505 8747-85173; www. wienmuseum.at), where Beethoven worked on his Eroica symphony during 1803–4. At weekends you can then stop off at **Villa Wertheimstein** (Döblinger Hauptstrasse 96; Sat 3.30pm–6pm, Sun 10am–noon; www.bezirksmuseum.at), a masterpiece of 19th-century Biedermeier architecture, full of period pieces, and featuring a lovely English garden.

At the end of the line (Heiligenstädter Park), walk across the park past the monument to Beethoven to Pfarrplatz 2, the prettiest of the composer's many Viennese homes. Take bus 38A to Probusgasse 6, the house where, in 1802, the composer penned his tragic *Heiligenstadt Testament*, in which he told his two brothers of his encroaching deafness. Today it is the **Beethoven Wohnung Heiligenstadt** (Tue–Sun 10am–1pm and 2–6pm; free entry on the first Sun of each month; www.wienmuseum.at).

THE HOHENSTRASSE

To explore the hills and woods that lie to the north of the city, take the 38A bus from Heiligenstadt U-Bahn up to the **Höhenstrasse** leading to Kahlenberg and Leopoldsberg on the northern slopes of the Wienerwald. The route offers a grandiose view of the city and surrounding country. You'll find it difficult to believe that you're still inside the city limits. If time permits, get out at one of the stops en route and have a walk around.

Near the end of the Hohenstrasse is the **Kahlenberg**. Since the end of the 18th century, the heights of Kahlenberg have been dotted with fashionable summer homes offering what is known as *Sommerfrische* (cool summer respite from the city heat). During two steaming hot days in July 1809, the Viennese aristocracy had a grandstand view of Napoleon's Battle of Wagram against the Austrians. Sipping cool Nussdorfer white wine, they watched the slaughter of 40,000 Austrians and 34,000 Frenchmen on the other side of the Danube.

The Höhenstrasse goes as far as **Leopoldsberg**, the very edge of the Wienerwald and the extreme eastern point of the European Alps. On a clear day, you can see about 100km (60 miles) eastwards from the terrace of the **Leopoldskirche** to the Carpathian Mountains in Slovakia.

KLOSTERNEUBURG

A short detour 7km (4 miles) to the north takes you to the imposing Augustine abbey of **Klosterneuburg** ⓸ (daily 9am– 6pm; U-Bahn 4 to Heiligenstadt and then bus 238 or 239; www. stift-klosterneuburg.at). A story claims it was founded by Duke Leopold III of Babenberg in 1106 on the spot where his bride's lost veil was discovered by his hunting dogs. In fact, its foundation is earlier, but little of the original edifice remains. Karl VI, who was very much taken with Spain, undertook major alterations in the 18th century, making it a baroque version of El Escorial. He wanted a combined palace and church with nine domes, each topped with a crown of the House of Habsburg. Only two were completed in his lifetime: the crown of the empire on the big dome and of the Austrian archduchy on the little one.

Klosterneuburg abbey

Klosterneuburg also features a museum of modern art, the **Essl Museum** (Tue,

Thur–Sun 10am–6pm, Wed until 9pm; www.sammlung-essl.at), a private foundation devoted to avant-garde Austrian artists and some of their American and European contemporaries.

The baroque ornamentation is indeed impressive, but the whole trip is made worthwhile by the **Leopoldskapelle**, with its magnificent **Verdun Altar** of 1181 containing 45 enamelled panels depicting scenes from the Scriptures. It served as a graphic Bible for the poor who could not read the stories.

Escaping the city

The sights around Vienna, from the Wienerwald to further afield in Burgenland, are all easily reached as a day trip from the city, using Austria's excellent network of public transport. The train (see www.oebb.at) will get you to most places, and those sights without a station will be served by connecting buses (see www.postbus.at).

THE WIENERWALD

While it can be seen along the Höhenstrasse, to appreciate the **Wienerwald** properly, you must visit the villages hidden away in the forest to the south and southwest of Vienna (for information on local buses and trains check on www.wienerlinien.at). First head out to Perchtoldsdorf, a serene little village amid heather-covered hills, vineyards and fir trees. Continue south to Burg Liechtenstein, a 'ruined castle' built in 1873 on the site of the 12th-century home of the Liechtenstein dynasty. The park is an ideal spot for a picnic. In **Mödling** you can see the 15th-century Gothic Spitalkirche (Hospital Church) and the house (Hauptstrasse 79) where Beethoven worked on his *Missa Solemnis*.

To the west is **Hinterbrühl**. Romantics like to believe that the picturesque mill, Höldrichsmühle (converted into an inn), is where Franz Schubert wrote songs for the miller's daughter Rosi (*Die schöne Müllerin*) in 1823. In fact the story originated in an 1864 operetta devoted to the composer's life. But the inn's wines can make believers of us all.

Beyond is the Sattelbach Valley and the Cistercian abbey of **Heiligenkreuz** (Holy Cross), founded in 1133. Heiligenkreuz is named after the relic of a piece of the True Cross, given to Austria by the King of Jerusalem in the 12th century and kept in the tabernacle behind the high altar. The courtyard features a **Trinity Column** (Pillar of the Plague), the work of baroque artist Giovanni Giuliani, who also designed the basilica's splendid choir stalls. The structure retains its Romanesque western facade. Along its south side is a graceful 13th-century cloister with 300 red columns.

In the town **churchyard** you'll find a tomb bearing the inscription: *'Wie eine Blume sprosst der Mensch auf und wird gebrochen'* ('Like a flower, the human being unfolds – and is broken'). This is the grave of Baroness Mary Vetsera, the 17-year-old who died in 1889 at nearby **Mayerling** in an apparent suicide pact with her lover Crown Prince Rudolf, heir to the Austro-Hungarian Empire. To hush the scandalmongers, the hunting lodge where the Mayerling tragedy occurred was demolished shortly thereafter and replaced with a Carmelite convent.

BADEN

From town the Badner Bahn (www.wlb.at) will take you from the Kärntner Ring to the romantic Helenental Valley and the spa of **Baden bei Wien**, 25km (16 miles) south of Vienna. Enjoyed by the Romans and made fashionable by Franz I in 1803, Baden became the very symbol of upright Viennese Biedermeier prosperity. The gentry of Vienna built their summer villas here and bathed in the 36°C (97°F) sulphurous waters. The thermal waters can still be enjoyed in the indoor pool (Brusattiplatz 4), open-air pools (Helenen Strasse 19–21) and mineral-water pools (Marchetti Strasse 13). Return via **Gumpoldskirchen**, a village with first-rate *Heuriger* wine gardens and not a bad place to stay if you want to be out of town (see page 139).

THE DANUBE VALLEY

If your visit gives you time for only one side-trip it should unquestionably be along the **Danube Valley ③**, in particular the magical area known as the Wachau between the historic towns of Melk and Krems. About an hour west of Vienna, this is where the Danube Valley is at its most scenic, by turns both charming and verdant with vineyards, apricot orchards and rustic villages, then suddenly forbidding with ruined medieval castles and rocky cliffs half hidden in mist. This is a landscape whose atmosphere is heavy with myth. Legend has it that the Burgundy kings of the medieval German epic, the *Nibelungenlied*, passed this spot en route to the kingdom of

The ruined 13th-century Burg Aggstein

the Huns. The crusaders also passed through here on their way to the Holy Land. Take the Danube River Steamer if you simply want to sit and dream as this mythical world passes you by. For a closer look at the towns and castles on the way it's best to travel by train or bus.

MELK

On a leisurely tour of the Danube Valley, 84km (52 miles) by the Westautobahn from Vienna, the Benedictine abbey of **Melk** ㉜ (Stift Melk; daily Apr–Oct 9am–5.30pm, Nov–Mar pre-booked guided tours only; www.stiftmelk.at) makes an ideal starting point. Towering high above the river on a pro-truding rock, this is one of the region's most majestic sights. Its position overlooking a bend in the river made this a strategic site from the time of the Romans. The Babenberg predecessors of the Habsburgs erected a fortress here in the 10th century, which they handed over to the Benedictines in 1106. The monks gradually created an abbey of huge proportions, enhanced by the baroque transformations of architect Jakob Prandtauer in 1702. Two towers, together with the octagonal dome and the lower Bibliothek (Library) and Marmorsaal (Marble Hall), form a harmonious group.

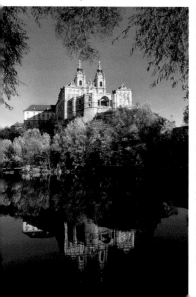

The abbey of Melk

The interior of the church is rich in reds and golds with a high altar by Antonio Beduzzi and superbly sculpted pulpit, choir and confessionals. The ceiling frescoes are by Johann Michael Rottmayr, whose work also adorns Vienna's Karlskirche.

Before crossing the Danube, make a quick detour to the village of **Mauer**, 10km (6 miles) due east of Melk, to see the late Gothic wooden altarpiece in the parish church. The work, by an anonymous local artist around 1515, depicts the Adoration of the Virgin Mary with a wealth of vivid detail.

MEDIEVAL TOWNS OF THE WACHAU

The Wachauer Strasse, along the north bank, is dotted with apricot orchards and vineyards, old *Weinhüterhütten* (vineguards' huts) and villages with *Heuriger* wine gardens.

On the opposite bank, you can see Schönbühel and the 13th-century ruins of **Burg Aggstein**. The castle was once owned by a robber baron named Jörg Scheck vom Wald, popularly known as 'Schreckenwald' (Terror of the Forest). One of his favourite activities was to lead prisoners to his rose garden, on the edge of a sheer precipice, where they were given the choice of either starving to death or ending it quickly by jumping 53m (175ft) onto the rocks below.

Back on the happier north bank, visit the town of **Spitz**, with its late Gothic **St Mauritius** church. It's known for its statues of the Apostles in the 1380 organ gallery, and the baroque painting of the Martyrdom of St Mauritius by Kremser (Martin Johann) Schmidt. In the village of **St Michael**, look for seven stone hares perched on the roof of the 16th-century church. These commemorate a particularly vicious winter when snowdrifts were said to have enabled the animals to jump clear over the church. In the village of **Weissenkirchen** is a fortified church, which was originally surrounded by four towers, a moat, ramparts and 44 cannons.

Prosperous Krems

The most romantic of these medieval towns is **Dürnstein**, famous as the site of Richard the Lion Heart's imprisonment in 1192–3. Devastated by the Swedish army in 1645, the castle of Kuenringer is more interesting to look at from below than it is to visit. But do make a point of seeing Dürnstein's **abbey church**, a baroque structure with a splendid carved wooden door to the abbey courtyard and an imposing statue of the resurrected Christ at the church entrance.

KREMS

Krems ❸ is the heart of the region's wine industry and historically one of the Danube Valley's most important trading centres. Today, you can enjoy its superb Gothic, Renaissance and baroque residences on tranquil, tree-shaded squares. Start on Südtiroler Platz and walk through the 15th-century Steiner Tor (Town Gate) with its Gothic pepper-pot towers. Turn left up Schmidgasse to Körnermarkt and the Dominikanerkirche (Dominican Church), transformed into an important museum of medieval art. Continue round to Pfarrplatz, dominated by the **Pfarrkirche**, a lovely church remodelled (1616–30) by two Italian architects and decorated with altar paintings by Franz Anton Maulbertsch and the masterful frescoes of Kremser Schmidt. The oldest square in Krems, Hoher Markt, features a masterpiece of Gothic residential architecture, the arcaded **Gozzoburg**, built around 1270. Take a stroll along the Untere Landstrasse to see some elegant baroque facades and the fine Renaissance **Rathaus** (Town Hall). On a contemporary note, a modern art museum has opened in the town, the **Kunsthalle Krems** (www.kunsthalle.at) and close by a **Karikaturmuseum** (www.karikaturmuseum.at). It includes work by the Austrian cartoonist Manfred Deix, who was renowned for being less than flattering to his fellow-countrymen.

Before leaving Krems, try some of the local 'new wine' served in one of the leafy courtyards along the Obere Landstrasse.

A SONG FOR RICHARD

During the Crusade of 1191, the brave but cheeky English king, Richard the Lionheart, enraged Leopold V von Babenberg by replacing the Austrian flag in Acre, Palestine, with the English one. Worse than that, he prevented the Austrians from sharing in the booty. But, on his way home, though dressed as a peasant, Richard was recognised and thrown into the darkest dungeon of Dürnstein Castle. He languished there for several years until the faithful minstrel Blondel came looking for him, singing a song known only to the king and himself. Richard revealed his place of imprisonment by joining in the chorus. His ransom, 23,000kg (22.6 tons) of silver, was enough to finance the Holy Roman Empire's expedition to Sicily and to build a new Ring Wall around Vienna.

TO THE EAST

Heading east from Vienna along the Danube traces the ancient eastern European boundary of the Roman Empire. About 36km (22 miles) from the city, at Petronell, are the remains of **Carnuntum**, which was once the capital of the Roman province of Pannonia (embracing much of modern Hungary and eastern Austria). In the 2nd century AD, under Hadrian and Marcus Aurelius, it was a thriving commercial centre. A summer festival is held in the Roman amphitheatre.

Five kilometres (3 miles) south of Petronell is **Rohrau**, the birthplace of Joseph Haydn. You can visit the beautifully restored thatched farmhouse where he was born in 1732. Concerts are held here during spring and summer. Nearby is the Schloss Rohrau, the baroque castle of the Harrach family, early patrons of young Haydn. The castle has a fine collection of 17th-century Spanish, Flemish and Italian art.

NEUSIEDLERSEE

Beyond Rohrau, and further east, is the **Neusiedler See** ㉞. This birdwatchers' paradise teems with heron, teal, water-fowl, wild geese and egret. The water of the lake is so shallow that it's possible to wade right across – only a few spots are more than 1.5m (5ft) deep. If you do cross, be aware that the southern end of the lake belongs to Hungary and you may need your passport. Flat-bottomed boats can be hired for fishing and in win-ter you can go skating and

Fishermen at Neusiedlersee

ice-sailing. Along the lake's western shores are the villages of **Rust** and **Mörbisch**, both famous for the storks that use local chimneys for nesting. Mörbisch, on the Hungarian border, is particularly attractive, and the wine gardens are simply marvellous.

EISENSTADT

The baroque town of **Eisenstadt** ㉟, 52km (32 miles) south of Vienna, is where Joseph Haydn worked from 1761 as musical director for the Hungarian prince Paul Esterházy. His house, the **Haydn-Haus** (www.haydn

Bergenkirche, where Haydn is laid to rest

haus.at), contains his collection of paintings, sheets of music and personal possessions. Haydn loved Eisenstadt and wanted to live and die here. He managed the living, but died in Vienna, without having taken the precaution of specifying where he wanted to be buried. Unfortunately, shortly after he was buried in Vienna in 1809, someone stole his skull, which was put on exhibition. The headless body was eventually returned to Eisenstadt where the skull rejoined it in 1954; both now lie reunited in a white marble grave at the **Bergenkirche**. The church is also noted for a Kalvarienberg, a Calvary display of life-size figures showing the stations of the cross, displayed in a series of austere dungeon-like rooms.

WHAT TO DO

ENTERTAINMENT

OPERA

It's difficult to think of a cultural institution in another European capital that holds the privileged place of the **Staatsoper** (National Opera; www.wiener-staatsoper.at) in Vienna. Since this is Austria, even those who loathe opera can be tempted in and converted. A Mozart performance is always a classic; while the more well-rounded opera-goers might take on Wagner or Alban Berg.

If you have tickets for a première or other gala performance, you should wear evening dress, though even on an ordinary night, people turn up in black tie or long dress. Jeans and shorts are a definite no-no.

First-rate opera and operetta can also be heard at the **Volksoper** (Währingerstrasse 78; www.volksoper.at), and opera and ballet at the **Theater an der Wien** (Linke Wienzeile 6; www.theater-wien.at).

MUSIC

Music is an integral part of Vienna. There really is something for everyone, with concerts held in historic buildings, including Schönbrunn and the Belvedere. However, the really serious music-making takes place in the city's famous concert halls, chief amongst them the **Musikverein** (Dumbastrasse 3; www.musikverein.at), now with four new halls. The other major hall is the **Konzerthaus** (Lothringestrasse 20; www. konzerthaus.at).

Festivals take place throughout the year, the most important being the **Wiener Festwochen** (www.festwochen.at)

Strauss statue in the Stadtpark

Performance in the Musikverein

in May and June. The festivals and concert seasons are showcases for the city's ensembles, including the **Wiener Philharmoniker** (www.wienerphilharmoniker.at), one of the world's finest orchestras. Other fine orchestras resident in the city include the **Wiener Symphoniker** (www.wiener-symphoniker.at), and the **Radio Symphonie Orchester Wien** (www.rso.orf.at). **Klang Forum Wien** (www.klangforum.at) specialises in contemporary music, while the **Concentus Musicus Wien** is one of Europe's most important early-music ensembles.

Of course, there are many opportunities to hear the music of composers associated with the city. In fact, the music of Mozart, Haydn, Schubert and Beethoven is performed in Vienna's oldest concert hall, the **Sala Terrena** (Singerstrasse 7; www.mozarthaus.at). You should also try to hear the celebrated **Wiener Sängerknaben** (Vienna Boys' Choir, www.wienersaengerknaben.at), who sing at Sunday Mass and other festivities in the Burgkapelle in the Hofburg.

THEATRE

The **Burgtheater** (National Theatre; Dr Karl Lueger-Ring 2; www.burgtheater.at) is not just Vienna's proudest theatre, but also one of the leading ensembles of the German-speaking world. The related **Akademietheater** (Lisztrasse 1) focuses on modern and avant-garde drama.

Performances are held all year round at Vienna's **English Theatre** at Josefsgasse 12 (www.englishtheatre.at). There are several English-speaking theatre groups in the city, and special performances are staged for children. Not far from here is the excellent **Josefstadt Theater** (Josefstädter Strasse 26; www.josefstadt.org) that always has interesting productions.

CINEMA

Austrian cinema has a long history, stretching back to the early years of silent film. Vienna itself has some excellent cinemas, including the **Filmmuseum** (www.filmmuseum.at), underneath the Albertina, that puts on screenings of classic European and English-language films. The **Burg Kino** on the Ringstrasse (www.burgkino.at) shows original-language English movies, as well as regular screenings of *The Third Man* (currently on Sundays at 2.20pm).

Elsewhere, the **Urania Kino** in the observatory at the end of the Stubenring (Uraniastrasse 1) has a nice auditorium, while the **Künstlerhaus Kino** (www.k-haus.at) on Karlsplatz is the place to catch avant-garde and art-house films, as well as being the venue for a number of film festivals.

Listings

Clubs come and go, so consult a copy of *Falter* (www.falter.at), the weekly listings magazine, for the latest information about nightclubs, parties and lounges.

NIGHTLIFE

The city is said to have more than 6,000 bars, nightclubs,

Night lights at the Donaukanal

discos and cabarets – with many of the most popular bars staying open round the clock. There are a few large clubs, but also many small venues with music provided by well-known DJs. There are cool lounge clubs, too, where people chill out to easy-listening sounds.

North of Stephansdom, the area around Ruprechtsplatz, Seitenstettengasse and Rabensteig forms the previously hot **Bermudadreieck** (Bermuda Triangle). Apart from the excellent **First Floor** bar (Seitenstettengasse 5; www.firstfloorbar. at), this area is now passé, and much of the action has passed on to the district around Naschmarkt and the railway arches along the **Hernalser Gürtel** (on the western edge of the 8th District). The district around **Bäckerstrasse** is also chic. The tacky nightclubs around **Kärntnerstrasse** cater largely to the tourist trade.

Over on the Donaukanal is one of Vienna's best-known clubs, **Flex** (www.flex.at), with a legendary sound system and top DJs as well as live bands. Other popular places include **Passage** (www.sunshine.at), literally under the Burgring and formed out of a converted underpass; and, in the 12th District, **U4** (www.u-4.at), a long-standing club and live music venue. Along the Gürtel the scene revolves around chic bars with DJs and some live music. Good places to check out include **Chelsea** (www.chelsea.co.at), occupying a converted railway arch and known for its pulsating live music; the hard-core electronic venue of **rhiz** (www.rhiz.org); and the more chic and laid-back **Q[kju:]** (www.kju-bar.at).

SHOPPING

Perhaps surprisingly, Vienna has a lot to offer for those keen to go shopping. Behind many of the city's grand façades – or at least those spaces that have not been snapped up by international chains – are quirky boutiques, elegant design shops or long-standing purveyors of luxury handmade goods, from shoes and *Tracht*, to cakes and pastries.

WHERE AND WHEN TO SHOP

The winding streets of Vienna's **Inner City** are a good place to start any shopping expedition. Although now increasingly dominated by international names, especially along **Graben**, **Kohlmarkt** and **Kärntnerstrasse**, there are still numerous interesting local places to ferret out. To the west of the Inner City, **Mariahilferstrasse** is the other main shopping area: a long series of shops which only peters out at the Westbahnhof. Other good shopping districts can be found in the **university district** (near the Votivkirche) and around **Siebensterngasse** and **Lindengasse** in Neubau (the 7th District). Shops tend to be open between 9am and 6pm on weekdays, closing at 5pm on Saturday. Most places remain shut on Sundays.

Shoppers on the Graben

WHAT TO BUY

For general fashion a good place to start is **Steffl**, a large department store (Kärntnerstrasse 19; www.steffl-vienna.at) with a large number of concessions for both well-established and younger designers. Otherwise have a wander through the **Ringstrassen Galerien** (www.ringstrassengalerien.com) nearby on the Kärtner Ring. In the 1st District most of the big name designers can be found around Kohlmarkt with some of the more interesting stuff to be found at the very funky **2006FEB01** (Plankengasse 3) or the offshoot from long-standing Austrian hat-makers Mühlbauer at **Mode** (Seilergasse 5). Further afield check out the boutiques on Lindengasse and for up-and-coming Austrian designers do not miss **PARK** on Mondscheingasse (No. 20; www.park.co.at) close by.

For beautifully made *Tracht* (traditional Austrian clothing still popular in Vienna), go to **Tostmann Trachten** (Schottengasse

Dried fruit at the Naschmarkt

31; www.tostmann.at) or **Loden-Plankl** (Michaeler-platz 6; www.loden-plankl.at).

Vienna can also boast two world-class shoemakers. Neither **Rudolf Scheer** (Bräu-nerstrasse 4; www.scheer.at) or **Ludwig Reiter** (Mölkersteig 1; www.ludwig-reiter.com) are cheap but their shoes are superbly crafted.

Classic Viennese designs are other items worth seeking out. For glass and porcelain,

Christmas market at the Rathaus

head to **Augarten** (Spiegel-gasse 3) and **Lobmeyer** (Kärntnerstrasse 26). Wiener Werkstätte textiles can be found at **Backhausen** (Kärntnerstrasse 6/4) who also have a museum of original works in the basement of the shop. For replicas of classic lamps and lighting, check out **Woka** (Palais Breuner, Singerstrasse 16). Good examples of contemporary Austrian design can be found at **artup** (Bauernmarkt 8).

As such an important centre for classical music, Vienna has a couple of excellent places to buy CDs and sheet music. **Gramola** (Graben 16) is the best place to find recordings, while **Doblinger** (Dorotheergasse 10) has a vast selection of scores.

For food and drink, head for the city's best market on **Nasch-markt** or the wonderful selection at **Julius Meinl** (Kohlmarkt 1). Seasonal specialities can be found in the Christmas markets that take place outside the Rathaus or the Spittelberg district. Wonderful patisserie can be found at confectioners such as **Demel** (Kohlmarkt 14) and **Gerstner** (Kärntnerstrasse 13), with what is claimed to be the original Sachertorte on sale at the **Sacher** (Philharmonikerstrasse 4).

ACTIVE PURSUITS

The easiest way to get rid of excess *strudel* is by going for a walk or run in one of the city's many **parks**. The largest of these is the Prater, but there are parks dotted all around the Ringstrasse that give you a chance to stretch your legs.

Cycling is an enjoyable way of getting around Vienna – and of escaping traffic snarls. Bicycles can be rented from any one of 160 Austrian railway stations. In Vienna, the three stations that rent bicycles are Westbahnhof, Wien Nord and Floridsdorf. You can return your bicycle to any participating Austrian railway station. The free *See Vienna by Bike* brochure from the Tourist Information Office lists bicycle hire firms, and also provides regional maps of cycling routes. See Vienna's spectacular hinterland by **hiking** along the well-marked paths of the Wienerwald. In the winter, these paths can be used for **cross-country skiing**.

The 21km (13-mile) beach of the Donauinsel provides outdoor **swimming**, along with facilities for **water skiing** and **windsurfing**. Döbling's **Krapfenwaldbad** is a fashionable outdoor swimming pool, complete with champagne bar. Most handsome of the indoor swimming pools is the **Amalienbad**, Reumannplatz 23, with *Jugendstil* decor and an old-fashioned steam bath and sauna.

Youth centre

For information about events and activities for young people (aged 13 to 26), contact Jugendinfo at Babenbergerstrasse 1 (Mon–Wed 2–7pm, Thur–Sat 1–6pm, tel: 01-4000-84 100; www.jugendinfowien.at).

Ice-skating carries on year-round in the Wiener Stadthalle, Vogelweidplatz 14, and during the winter in Rathausplatz outside the town hall.

You can see professional football in the Prater, home of one the city's first division teams, Austria Vienna.

CHILDREN'S VIENNA

Vienna is a good destination for children. **Schönbrunn** (see page 66) has a number of distractions: there is the **Marionette Theatre** and maze, and a cellar devoted to the baking and tasting of *strudel*. There's also a **zoo** at Schönbrunn and a **vivarium** at Esterhazy Park. Also try the **Butterfly House** at Burggarten, and, for those who like stars, the city's **Planetarium** (Oswald Thomas Platz; www.planetarium-wien.at). Outside the city, on the eastern slopes of the Wienerwald, the **Lainz Wildlife Park** (www.lainzer-tiergarten.at) offers carriage rides, forest playgrounds, nature trails and even close-up encounters with wild boar.

Kids at Schönbrunn

The ZOOM Kindermuseum (www.kindermuseum.at) is specifically for children, while the Museum of Modern Art Ludwig Foundation, Museum of Fine Arts and Museum of Natural History all have children's programmes, and the Technical Museum and the House of Music both have lots to discover.

The **Prater funfair**, the **Spanish Riding School** (see page 44) and the view from the **Donauturm** (see page 71) are all must-sees and sure to captivate children. Playgrounds and beaches can be found on **Danube Island**. In summer, the **boats** on the Danube sometimes have children's events (www.ddsg-blue-danube.at).

CALENDAR OF EVENTS

For information and ticket details, contact the Tourist Information Office, tel: 01-24555, or consult www.wien.info.

January Vienna Philharmonic's traditional *Neujahrskonzert* (New Year's Day concert), 11am at Musikverein; jazz-lovers' alternative: Vienna Art Orchestra, 9pm at Sofiensäle, Marxergasse 17.

February/March *Opernball* (Opera Ball), at Staatsoper, the social event of the year; the *Ball der Philharmoniker* (Philharmonic Ball), at Musikverein, rivals the *Opernball* for prestige; *Fasching* (Carnival) procession in Döbling.

April *Ostermarkt* (Easter Market): a country-fair atmosphere on Freyung in Innere Stadt; *Wiener Sängerknaben* (Vienna Boys' Choir) weekly Mass in the Hofburg's Burgkapelle; *OsterKlang Wien* (Vienna's Sounds of Easter) music festival; Vienna Marathon accompanied by popular festivities.

May Traditional May Day celebrations at Prater amusement park; the Life Ball, an AIDS charity event supported by international celebrities.

June *Wiener Festwochen* (Vienna Festival), featuring music, dance and theatrical productions at Theater an der Wien and Messepalast; Regenbogen (Gay Rainbow) Parade on Ringstrasse; *Donaueninselfest* (Danube Island Festival), with funfair festivities; Donauinsel pop music festival, a free weekend event.

July/August *Jazzfest Wien* (Vienna Jazz Festival) at Staatsoper and Burgtheater; *Wiener Musiksommer*, summer festival of popular opera and operetta at Theater an der Wien; jazz, rock, reggae and hip-hop music festival at Wiesen, south of Vienna.

September Schönbrunn Palace festival; In-line Skating Marathon on the Ringstrasse.

October Viennale Film Festival; *Wean Hean* folk festival.

November/December *Christkindlmarkt* (Christmas Market) at Rathausplatz, Schönbrunn, Freyung, Spittelberg: carols, roast chestnuts, *Glühwein* and stalls laden with gifts; MuseumsQuartier courtyard decked with lights and decorations; concerts, recitals throughout the Innere Stadt; New Year's Eve *Kaiserball* (Emperor's Ball) in Hofburg.

EATING OUT

When it comes to Viennese cuisine, it is worth bearing in mind that this city was once the centre of the old Habsburg Empire of 60 million Eastern and Southern Europeans. The emperor and his archdukes and generals have gone, but not the Bohemian dumplings, the Hungarian goulash, the Polish stuffed cabbage and Serbian *schaschlik*, nor the plum, cherry and apricot brandies that accompany the Turkish coffee. And all are now frequently served with the lighter touch of the New Viennese Cuisine.

Dining out has always been a popular pastime in Vienna. It is part of Austrian culture to take the family out for lunch at the weekend and to meet friends in a *Beisl* (convivial Viennese equivalent of the bistro) or at the *Heuriger* wine garden. In restaurants, the emphasis is on good company, good wine, robust portions and, usually, reasonable prices for the quality of the ingredients – a dramatically different approach from many other European capitals.

When choosing a restaurant, something to bear in mind during the summer months is whether you can sit outside in a garden or *Schanigarten* (tables on the pavement with sunshades).

Drinking coffee on Mariahilferstrasse

A Wurststand (sausage stand) in the city

If you're simply after a quick snack, then look for a traditional *Würstelstand*, a small kiosk selling sausages and other local specialities, such as *Leberkäsesemmel* (liver pâté sandwich). These kiosks are open almost all day and are to be found on street corners all over the city.

VIENNESE FARE

Two Viennese staples that you're likely to come across immediately are the *Wienerschnitzel* and the *Backhendl*. The *Wienerschnitzel* is a large, thinly sliced cutlet of veal crisply sautéed in a coating of flour, egg and seasoned breadcrumbs. *Backhendl* is roast chicken prepared in the same way. Viennese gourmets insist that the *Wienerschnitzel* be served with cold potato or cucumber salad. You should also make sure that it is a cut of veal (*vom Kalb*) and not pork (*vom Schwein*), as in some of the cheaper establishments. The *Backhendl* is sometimes served with *Geröstete* (sautéed potatoes).

Tafelspitz (boiled beef) was Emperor Franz Joseph's favourite dish, and to this day is a form of ambrosia to the Viennese. Spice it up with *Kren* (horseradish) and *Schnittlauchsauce* (chive sauce). Another delight, originally from Hungary, is goulash – beef chunks stewed with onion, garlic, paprika, tomatoes and celery. *Debreziner* sausages, *Köménymagleves Nokedival* (caraway-seed soup with dumplings) and apple soup are three more Hungarian specialities.

From the Czech Republic comes Prague ham and *sauerkraut* soup; from Polish Galicia, roast goose; and from Serbia, peppery barbecued *cevapcici* meatballs and *schaschlik* brochettes of lamb with onions and green and red peppers.

Dumplings *(Knödel)*, made from flour, yeast or potatoes, are an Austrian staple. The *Marillenknödel* is a dessert dumpling, made of potato with a piping hot apricot inside. Another delicious dessert dumpling is the *Topfenknödel*, made with a cream-cheese filling.

Hot desserts are, in fact, a speciality, and you should also try *Buchteln* or *Wuchteln*, yeast buns often filled with plum

VIENNESE SAUSAGE STANDS

They all go for it: society ladies in posh frocks, night owls, opera buffs, workers – they all stand together at the Sausage Stand. Typical fare includes frankfurters (usual hot dog sausage), *Debreziner* (thin and spicy), *Bratwurst* (hunky thick fried sausage) and *Kasekrainer* (thick and made with meat and cheese). *Burenwurst* is a sort of boiled *Bratwurst*. There are stands all over town, including: **Albertina Wurstelstand**, Augustinerplatz, 8am–4am; **Hoher Markt** (the most famous), Marc Aurel Strasse, 7am–4am; and **Zur Oper**, Kärntnerstrasse, 10am–5am.

jam, and from Hungary the *Palatschinken*, pancakes filled with jam or nuts. And don't forget the *Apfelstrudel*, a flaky pastry filled with thinly sliced apples, raisins and cinnamon.

Finally, there's one of the most famous and sinfully delicious chocolate cakes in the world, the *Sachertorte*. Join in the endless debate over whether or not it should be split into two layers and where the apricot jam should go.

WINES AND WINE GARDENS

Wine in Vienna is almost always white, which the Viennese drink with meat and fish alike. The best known of Austrian white wines, the *Gumpoldskirchner*, has the full body and bouquet of its southern vineyards. The Viennese give equal favour to their own *Grinzinger*, *Nussdorfer*, *Sieveringer* and *Neustifter*. From the Danube Valley, with an extra natural sparkle, come the *Kremser*, *Dürnsteiner* and *Langenloiser*.

Of the reds, the *Vöslauer*, produced in Bad Vöslau near Baden, and the *Kalterersee*, imported from South Tyrol (Italy's Alto Adige region), are about the best. *Blaufränkisch* and *Zweigelt* are also reliable standbys.

To enjoy these wines in their original state, they should be ordered *herb* (dry). Often the producers will sweeten them for the foreign palate unless you specify otherwise. Perhaps the most pleasant thing about Viennese wine is the way in which it is drunk.

A Viennese vineyard

The Viennese have created a splendid institution, the *Heuriger*, where you can sip white wine on mild evenings under the stars.

Waitress service at Café Demel

Winemakers are allowed by law to sell a certain amount of their new wine (also called *Heuriger*) directly to the public. They announce the new wine by hanging out a sprig of pine over the door and a sign saying *Ausg'steckt* (open). The *Heuriger* of **Grinzing** are extremely popular, but many of the best ones are out in **Nussdorf**, **Ober-Sievering** and **Neustift**. *Heuriger* gardens are generally open from mid-afternoon until late in the evening and at weekends for lunch. The season runs from March to October.

The local *Gösser* beer presents a fair challenge to the powerful *Pilsner Urquell* imported from the Czech Republic. Among the brandies you should try the Hungarian *Barack* (apricot) and Serbian *Slivovitz* (plum).

COFFEE AND THE KAFFEEHAUS
The varieties of coffee in Vienna are virtually endless, and there are names for every shade from black to white. Ask for *einen kleinen Mokka* and you'll get a small, strong black

Delicious Sachertorte

coffee and stamp yourself as someone of French or Italian taste. A *Kapuziner*, topped with generous dollops of cream, is more Viennese; *ein Brauner*, with just a dash of milk, is as Viennese as can be. *Eine Melange* (pronounced 'melanksch'), a mixture of milk and coffee, is designed for sensitive stomachs; *ein Einspänner*, with whipped cream in a tall glass, is for aunts on Sundays; *ein Türkischer*, prepared semi-sweet in a copper pot, is for addicts of the Balkan Connection.

The Viennese *Kaffeehaus* dates back to the 17th century when, depending on which legend you choose, either a Polish spy named Kulczycki or a Greek merchant named Theodat opened the first café with a stock of coffee beans captured from the Turks. By the time of Maria Theresa the town was full of coffee houses, fashionable and shady, where gentry and intellectuals mingled. Some developed their own particular clientele – writers, artists, politicians – while the most prominent (Griensteidl, Café Central, Herrenhof) attracted all types.

After a post-war lull, the institution made a grand come-back. In the Innere Stadt, the renovated **Café Central** and the more sedate **Griensteidl** are thriving once again. With chandeliers adorning the ceiling, the former imperial bakery **Café Demel** on the Kohlmarkt is said to have the best cakes in town. **Café Hawelka**, at Dorotheergasse 6, once popular with artists and antiques dealers, has become a hangout for the younger crowd. Artists now prefer **Alt-Wien**, at Bäckerstrasse 9, and the **Kleines Café**, Franziskanerplatz 3, with its superb interior design by architect Hermann Czech. Intellectuals have followed the example of the late Thomas Bernhard in favouring **Café Bräunerhof**, at Stallburggasse 2. This café is also popular with music-lovers for its weekend chamber-music recitals. In the 6th District, **Café Sperl**, Gumpendorfer Strasse 11, is an elegant 100-year-old establishment complete with marble tables, *Jugendstil* chairs and an endless row of newspapers (including *The Times*, *Le Monde* and *La Stampa*).

TO HELP YOU ORDER...

Waiter, waitress, please! **Bedienung, bitte!**
Could we have a table? **Wir hätten gerne einen Tisch.**
May I see the menu, please? **Die Speisekarte, bitte.**
The bill please. **Zahlen bitte.**
I would like... **Ich möchte gerne...**

Beer **ein Bier**	Fruit juice **Fruchtsaft**
Bread **Brot**	Ice cream **Eis**
Butter **Butter**	Meat **Fleisch**
Cheese **Käse**	Menu **Speisekarte**
Dessert **Nachtisch**	Milk **Milch**
Fish **Fisch**	Mineral water
Fruit **Obst**	**Mineralwasser**

Potatoes **Erdäpfel**
Salad **Salat**
Soup **Suppe**
Sugar **Zucker**
Tea **Tee**
Wine **Wein**

...AND READ THE MENU

Kaiser-fleisch cured
  pork spare ribs
Kaiser schmarrn
  pancake with fruit
  compote
Kalb veal
Kirschen cherries
Knödeln dumplings
Kuchen cake
Lamm lamb
Leber liver
Marillen-knödel apricot
  dumpling
Nockerln small
  dumplings
Paradieser tomatoes
Rahm cream
Rindfleisch beef
Rostbraten pot roast
Rotkraut red cabbage
Schinken ham
Schweine-fleisch pork
Topfen cream cheese
Zwetschken plums
Zwiebeln onions

The latest news in a Vienna café

Auflauf casserole
Backhendl sautéed
  chicken
Debreziner spicy
  sausage
Ente duck
Erdbeeren strawberries
Faschiertes minced
  meat
Frittaten suppe broth
  with sliced crêpes
Gans goose
Guglhupf coffee cake
Gurke gherkin

PLACES TO EAT

*Restaurants are listed alphabetically. Price categories are based
on the cost, per person, of a dinner comprising starter, mid-
priced main course and dessert (not including wine, coffee, or
service) and are indicated as follows:*

€€€ over 40 euros   **€€** 15–40 euros   **€** 15 euros and under

Cafés serve meals in the **€** category unless otherwise specified.

RESTAURANTS

THE INNERE STADT (DISTRICT 1)

Al Borgo €€ *1, An Der Hulben 1, tel: 01-512 8559, open Mon–Fri
11.30am–3pm, 6pm–midnight, Sat 6pm–midnight, www.alborgo.at.*
Specialising in Mediterranean cuisine, Al Borgo's chef serves Italian specialties with a creative twist, using only top-quality fresh
local ingredients. An ever-changing seasonal menu.

Artner am Franziskanerplatz €€–€€€ *1, Franziskanerplatz 5, tel:
01-503 5034, open Mon–Sat noon–midnight, www.artner.co.at.* Sister
restaurant to the more experimental Artner in the 4th district, this
eatery plates up some wonderful Austrian fare, including regional
specialities from Styria. Finish off with a Burgenland wine, served
in an atmospheric brick-lined cellar with a chic interior design.

Beim Czaak €–€€ *1, Postgasse 15, tel: 01-513 7215, open Mon–Sat
4pm–midnight, www.czaak.com.* A friendly *Beisl* with helpful staff
tucked away behind the Old University, hence popular with students. The hearty menu includes superb *Tafelspitz*, sinful desserts
and an excellent selection of beers.

Bristol Lounge €€€ *1, Kärntner Ring 1, tel: 01-5151 6553, open
daily 7am–midnight; www.bristol-lounge.at.* Conveniently located
next to the Vienna Opera, Bristol Hotel's restaurant enjoys a lovely
historic Art Déco ambiance. Chef Manuel Gratzl serves excellent
traditional Austrian dishes and imaginative interpretations of international classics. Live piano music. Cosy winter garden.

Cantinetta Antinori €€–€€€ *1, Jasomirgottstrasse 3–5, tel: 01-5337 722, open daily 11.30am–midnight,* www.cantinetta-antinori.com. Run by the famous Tuscan wine-producing family, this is a slick Italian restaurant serving reliable food. Closely packed tables are not for the shy. The Chianti wines produced by the owners are a must.

Coburg €€€ *1, Coburgbastei 4, tel: 01-5181 80, open daily 7pm–midnight,* www.palais-coburg.com. One of the best places to eat in the city in a rather classy palace hotel. Opened in 2002 by chef Christian Petz, the Coburg dishes up great Austrian classics with a twist, and there is an amazing selection of wines (the cellar has over 50,000 bottles).

Esterhazy Keller € *1, Haarhof 1, tel: 01-533 3482, open Mon–Fri 4–11pm, Sat–Sun 11am–11pm.* A *Stadtheurigen* in a dark cellar; take the winding stairs down from the small doorway. Typical belt-stretching food and local wines. Atmospheric in a very Viennese sort of way.

Gasthaus Pöschl €–€€ *1, Weihburggasse 17, tel: 01-513 5288, open daily noon–midnight (kitchen closes 10.45pm).* Popular at lunchtime with local workers, it serves up tasty home-cooked traditional Austrian fare and has a good range of drinks.

Griechenbeisl €€ *1, Fleischmarkt 11, tel: 01-533 1977, open daily 11am–1am,* www.griechenbeisl.at. This tavern was first recorded in 1447 and its small vaulted rooms have been a public house ever since. First frequented by Levantine and Greek merchants (hence the name), who inhabited Fleishmarkt, it was subsequently visited by many famous musicians and writers. Now the classic Viennese food is largely served up to tourists.

Gulaschmuseum € *1, Schulerstrasse 20, tel: 01-512 1017, open daily 11am–midnight.* Goulash is as popular in Austria as in its native Hungary. At the 'Goulash Museum' you can choose from a whole range of exceedingly tasty meat dishes, though there are also vegetarian versions.

Hansen €€ *1, Wipplingerstrasse 34, tel: 01-532 0542, open Mon–Fri 9am–11pm, Sat 9am–5pm,* www.hansen.co.at. Set in the vaulted cellars underneath Theophil Hansen's Borse building, and sharing the space with the florist Lederleitner, this is a lovely place for a meal. The food is modern Mediterranean with a slight Austrian twist and it is a great place for breakfast (served until 11.30am).

Loca €€€ *1, Stubenbastei 1, tel: 01-512 1172, open daily 5pm–midnight*. The six-course surprise tasting menu is really worth a try and is perfectly paired with wine.

Meinl's €€€ *1, Graben 19, tel: 01-5323 3346 000, open Mon–Fri 8am–midnight, Sat 9am–midnight, www.meinlamgraben.at*. Taking advantage of its place above Vienna's most prestigious food store, the eponymous Meinl serves up good reinvented Austrian classics and excellent wines.

Palmenhaus €€ *1, Burggarten, tel: 01-533 1033, open Mon–Thur 11am–midnight, Fri 10am–midnight, Sat 9am–midnight, Sun 9am–11pm, www.palmenhaus.at*. This spectacular *Jugendstil* glasshouse now houses a restaurant and café. Good modern European dishes and a few Viennese classics although things can get quite crowded and noisy the later it gets.

Pfudl €–€€ *1, Bäckerstrasse 22, tel: 01-512 6705, open daily 10am–midnight, www.gasthauspfudl.com*. This *Beisl* has a rural atmosphere and finely prepared traditional Viennese cuisine, topped off with speedy service and a meagre bill.

Plachutta €€–€€€ *1, Wollzeile 38, tel: 01-512 1577, open daily 11.30am–midnight (kitchen closes 11.15pm), www.plachutta.at*. A long-standing central restaurant that is particularly famous for its *Tafelspitz* although the other Viennese classics are not bad either.

Reinthaler €€ *1, Dorotheergasse 2, Gluckgasse 5, tel: 01-513 1249/01-512 3366, open (Dorotheergasse) daily 11am–11pm, (Gluckgasse) Mon–Fri 9am–11pm*. Classic city-centre *Beisl*, very popular with the Viennese for the hearty portions and quality of the food.

Salonplafond im MAK €€–€€€ *1, Stubenring 5, tel: 01-226 0046, open daily 10am–2am, www.salonplafond.wien*. The café and restaurant of the Museum of Applied Arts has been beautifully designed and turns out excellent modern takes on classic Austrian dishes as well as a good selection of wines. DJ music.

Trzesniewski € *1, Dorotheergasse 1, tel: 01-512 3291, open Mon–Fri 8.30am–7.30pm, Sat 9am–6pm, Sun 10am–5pm, www.trzesniewski. at*. With a great preserved interior this place specialises in the beloved Viennese open-faced sandwich, with toppings such as egg, red onion, salmon or crab. Diners cluster around chest-high tables and eat standing up; beer is the drink of choice here.

Wrenkh €€ *1, Bauernmarkt 10, tel: 01-533 1526, open Mon–Sat noon–10pm, www.wrenkh-wien.at*. A place for vegetarians and healthy eaters with top-notch food, excellent wines and a cosy ambience.

Zu den 3 Hacken €–€€ *1, Singerstrasse 28, tel: 01-512 5895, open Mon–Sat 11am–midnight, www.vinum-wien.at*. A good place for lovers of traditional Viennese cooking. The menu is big, and so are the portions. Very popular with local diners, so advance booking may be necessary.

Zum Schwarzen Kameel € *1, Bognergasse 5, tel: 01-5338 12511, open daily 8am–midnight, www.kameel.at*. This delicatessen and Art Nouveau restaurant is crammed with history – allegedly Beethoven used to eat here, though he probably wouldn't recognise today's gourmet menu which locals flock to savour.

AROUND THE RINGSTRASSE (DISTRICTS 2–9)

Entler €€€ *4, Schlusselgasse 2, tel: 01-504 3585, www.entler.at*. Not far from the Taubstummengasse metro station, this highly recommended restaurant combines contemporary and traditional décor to set the perfect scene for some of the capital's best Austrian cuisine. Service is top-notch but be prepared to wait a little for your food as everything is prepared fresh.

Gasthaus Wild €€ *3, Radetzkyplatz 1, tel: 01-920 9477, open daily 9am–1am*. This *Beisl* has been beautifully restored, keeping the original character. The food, which includes typical Viennese dishes, is excellent, as is the selection of beers and wines.

Glacis Beisl €€ 7, *Breitegasse 4, tel: 01-526 5660, open daily 11am–2pm*, www.glacisbeisl.at. Part of the MuseumsQuartier complex, a busy modern space that serves up great Viennese food. Very popular so it's advisable to book.

Schnattl €€€ 8, *Lange Gasse 40, tel: 01-405 3400, open Mon–Thur 11.30am–5pm, Fri 11.30am–midnight*, www.schnattl.com. Top contemporary Austrian cuisine bursting with fresh and delicate flavours. The interior is a pleasant and airy traditional space and the selection of wines is superb.

Schweizerhaus € 2, *Prater 116, tel: 01-728 01520, open mid-Mar–Oct, daily 11am–11pm*, www.schweizerhaus.at. Huge portions of belly-extending roast pork knuckle (known as *Stelze*) served up in a madly busy eating house; you can also relax with a draught beer in the tree-shaded garden.

Silberwirt €–€€ 5, *Schlossgasse 21, tel: 01-544 4907, open daily noon–midnight*, www.silberwirt.at. This very popular *Beisl* is packed at weekends with all kinds of folk. Good, traditional fare served up in a charming courtyard setting, all at a decent price.

Steirereck im Wien €€€ 3, *Am Heumarkt 2a, tel: 01-713 3168, open (restaurant) Mon–Fri 11.30am–2.30pm, 6.30–10pm*, www.steirereck.at. One of Austria's top restaurants, now relocated to a beautifully designed modern building overlooking the Stadtpark. It specialises in creative twists on Austrian classics. Try the cheaper lunch menu, or sample the huge range of cheeses in the Meierei.

Witwe Bolte €–€€ 7, *Gutenberggasse 13, tel: 01-523 1450, open daily 11.45am–11.30pm*, www.witwebolte.at. Viennese home-style cooking at its best in one of the city's oldest and simplest *Beisln*. Located in the interesting Spittleberg district.

FURTHER AFIELD

Braunsperger Roland Kroiss €–€€ 19, *Sieveringer Strasse 108, tel: 01-320 3992, open daily Jan and alternate months 3.30pm–late*. If you have a particular interest in genuine local grape varieties, then don't miss this *Heuriger*. *Weissburgunder, roter Zweigelt* and *Grüner*

Veltliner are among those on offer, while *Gemischter Satz* is a blend of different grape varieties that are picked and pressed together.

Fuhrgassl-Huber €–€€ *19, Neustift am Walde 68, tel: 01-440 1405, open Mon–Sat 2pm–midnight, Sun, holidays noon–midnight, www.fuhrgassl-huber.at.* If you fancy a rustic setting, don't miss the earthy atmosphere of this *Heuriger*. On days when it's too cold to sit outside in the magnificent garden, warm yourself indoors with a plate of suckling pig, grilled chicken or other choice items from the buffet.

Gerhard Klager €–€€ *21, Stammersdorfer Strasse 14, tel: 01-292 4107, open daily 1pm–midnight, every other month.* This *Heuriger* is particularly good for children, who can play in the playground while the adults sample fine wines and high-quality food. If you're driving, try the delicious low-alcohol version.

VIENNESE CAFÉS

Aida *1, Singerstrasse 1, tel: 01-890 8988-210, open Mon–Fri 7am–10pm, Sat–Sun 8am–10pm, www.aida.at.* Aida is a chain themed in shocking pink with 1950s decor. The coffee is wonderful (some say the best) and the *patisserie* is a dream.

Alt Wien *1, Bäckerstrasse 9, tel: 01-512 5222, open daily 10am–2am, www.kaffeealtwien.at.* A café bordering on a *Beisl* with a deliberately decadent and dingy atmosphere. It offers a mouth-watering selection of snacks. You may come across an interesting literary clientele in the evenings.

Bräunerhof *1, Stallburggasse 2, tel: 01-512 3893, open Mon–Fri 8am–8.30pm, Sat 8am–6.30pm, Sun 10am–6.30pm.* Popular city-centre café with a wide selection of *Torten*.

Café Central *1, Herrengasse 14 (Palais Ferstel), tel: 01-533 3763 24, open Mon–Sat 7.30am–10pm, Sun and holidays 10am–10pm, www.palaisevents.at.* The haunt of artists and intellectuals from times past, including Leon Trotsky and Peter Altenberg. Now a bit of a tourist trap and pricey.

Café Drechsler *6, Linke Wienzeile 22, tel: 01-581 2044, open Mon–Thur and Sun 8am–midnight, Fri–Sat 8am–2am*, www.cafedrechsler. at. This round-the-clock café has been providing hot comfort to the market traders across the road for years. The food is good and so are the prices.

Demel k.u.k Hofzuckerbäcker *1, Kohlmarkt 14, tel: 01-535 1717, open daily 9am–7pm*, www.demel.at. Candies, crowds and cakes since 1796. Demel was, by appointment, pastry chef to Franz Joseph. It serves some of the best cakes in town.

Diglas *1, Wollzeile 10, tel: 01-5125 7650, open 8am–10.30pm*, www.diglas.at. A venerable coffee house with very comfortable seats and huge slabs of cake. One of the city's best and conveniently located near Stephansplatz.

Frauenhuber *1, Himmelpfortgasse 6, tel: 01-512 5353, open Mon–Sat 8am–midnight, Sun and holidays 10am–10pm*, www.cafefrauen huber.at. One of Vienna's oldest cafés (1824) and one of the prettiest. It's said that Mozart performed here and Beethoven was a regular.

Griensteidl *1, Michaelerplatz 2, tel: 01-5352 6920, open 8am–11.30pm*. Light and airy café in traditional style, by the Hofburg.

Hawelka *1, Dorotheergasse 6, tel: 01-512 8230, open Mon–Wed 8am–midnight, Thur–Sat 8am–1am, Sun and holidays 10am–midnight*. A dark and atmospheric café with a central location but today without its former artist patrons.

Kleines Café *1, Franziskanerplatz 3, no telephone, open Mon–Sat 10am–2am, Sun 1pm–2am*. As the name suggests this is a tiny place, but beautifully designed and popular with local intellectuals. There is overspill outside in the square during summer.

Landtmann *1, Universitätsring 4, tel: 01-241 00100, open 7.30am–midnight*, www.landtmann.at. Always the most prestigious of the Ringstrasse cafés, next door to the Burgtheater.

Mozart *1, Albertinaplatz 2, tel: 01-241 00200, open daily 8am–*

midnight, www.cafe-mozart.at. There's been a café here since 1794. In Biedermeier times it was a meeting place for artists.

Museum *1, Operngasse 7, tel: 01-2410 0620, open daily 8am–midnight.* Popular with arts students and lecturers, with a disastrously over-renovated Adolf Loos interior.

Prückel *1, Stubenring 24, tel: 01-512 6115, open daily 8.30am–10pm.* Situated opposite the Museum of Fine Arts, this is a fine old Viennese café, with a 1950s interior, serving a full menu.

Sperl *6, Gumpendorfer Strasse 11, tel: 01-586 4158, open Mon–Sat 7am–11pm, Sun 11am–8pm.* Popular with Franz Lehár, and the meeting place of the stars, Sperl still attracts theatre people and literary types. Billiards and card tables.

Ubl *4, Pressgasse 26, tel: 01-587 6437, open Wed–Sun noon–2pm, 6pm–midnight.* Old-fashioned establishment serving good quality Schnitzels and other classic Austrian fare, including *Zwiebelrostbraten* and *Tafelspitz*.

A-Z TRAVEL TIPS

A Summary of Practical Information

A

ACCOMMODATION (For Recommended Hotels, see page 132)

The Vienna Tourist Board (www.wien.info) publishes a list of hotels, *Pensionen* (guest houses) and *Saison Hotels* (student hostels used as hotels from July to September) with details about amenities, prices and classifications. You can pick it up, along with a free city map, from the Austrian Tourist Board in your country or from travel agents. Tourist information offices in Vienna (see page 129) can book rooms for you, for a small fee. Be aware that if you cancel your reservation, all hotels have the right to charge a cancellation fee.

The more homely atmosphere of a pension in Vienna makes it popular for longer stays, though, as with some of the cheaper hotels, not all of them have rooms with private baths. Apartments are also available for longer stays. It is always advisable to book ahead, especially for travel from Easter to the end of September, and at Christmas and New Year. It is also possible to stay in private homes on a bed-and-breakfast basis. This is an especially attractive option in some of the smaller villages around Vienna. The famous old luxury hotels around the Opera are often fully booked by a long-established clientele, so reservations are necessary well in advance.

a guest house **eine Pension**
a single/double room **ein Einzel-/Doppelzimmer**
with/without bath (shower) **mit/ohne Bad (Dusche)**
What's the rate per night? **Was kostet eine Übernachtung?**

AIRPORT *(Flughafen)*

Vienna's airport, **Wien-Schwechat Airport** (VIE, www.viennaairport. com) is located about 20km (12 miles) from the centre of Vienna and handles domestic as well as international flights.

The City Airport Train (CAT, www.cityairporttrain.com), which leaves every 30 minutes, provides a high-speed (16 minutes) connection to the City Air Terminal at Landstrasse (Wien Mitte). There is also the Schnellbahn (S-Bahn), which takes longer but is much cheaper. Airport shuttle buses leave every 30 minutes for major transport hubs in the city centre. The Airport Service Wien is a private shuttle service that takes you to your exact address (tel: 676 351 6420, www.airportservice.at). A taxi to the city centre should cost around €35–40.

Where can I find a taxi? **Wo finde ich ein Taxi?**
How much is it to the centre? **Wieviel kostet es ins Zentrum?**
Does this bus go to the railway station? **Fährt dieser Bus zum Bahnhof?**

B

BICYCLE RENTAL *(Fahrrad-Verleih)*
Bicycles are available to rent from bike hire shops and at mainline railway stations. Pedal Power (Ausstellungsstrasse 3, www.pedal power.at) hires out bikes and organises guided tours (advance booking required) as does Vienna Explorer (Haidmannsgasse 8, www.viennaexplorer.com). Expect to pay around €30 a day, about 30 percent less if you are a student.

BUDGETING FOR YOUR TRIP
When budgeting for a trip to Vienna, count on most things being a touch more expensive than in the UK. However, this depends on the exchange rate between the pound and the euro.

A great way to save money is to buy a **Vienna Card** which provides reduced admission and other benefits at 210 museums and sights, theatres, concert halls, shops, restaurants, cafés and wine gardens *(Heuriger)*; unlimited travel by underground, bus and tram, and a reduction on the shuttle bus to/from the city centre.

The card valid for 48 hours costs €18.90 while the 72-hour card costs €21.90. It can be purchased at Vienna Airport and at hotels and tourist information offices (www.wien.info).

To give you an idea of what you can expect to pay for what, here is a short list of average prices. They can only be approximate, however, as in Austria, too, inflation creeps relentlessly up.

Hotels. (double room with bath or shower per night, including breakfast). ***** €200–750, **** €150–250, *** €100–200,** €80–150, * €50–100 (see Recommended Hotels, page 132).

Meals. The average cost of a standard meal, including a glass of wine is between €20 and €25 per person.

Museums. Entrance fees vary considerably. Concessions are available at many museums for holders of the Vienna Card. Entrance for children under six is free. There is a reduction for schoolchildren (passport required) and students (international student identity card required).

Public transport. €2.20 for single ticket, €7.60 for a 24-hour ticket, €16.50 for a 72-hour ticket. Children under six years old travel free.

C

CAMPING

For information about campsites, camping and caravanning, www.campsite.at is a helpful place to start. Of camping sites located around the city, one is open all year: Wien West I/II, Hüttelbergstrasse 40 and 80, tel: 914 2314. Other good camping sites are: Aktiv Camping Neue Donau, Am Kleehäufel, tel: 202 4010 (mid-May–Sept); Wien Süd, Breitenfurter Strasse 269, tel: 867 3649 (July–Aug). The website www.wiencamping.at contains useful information about all three sites.

CAR RENTAL/HIRE (*Autovermietung*, see also Driving)

For travelling inside the city, parking would make a car more of a hindrance than an asset, but having a car is certainly useful for excursions out to the Wienerwald and the Danube Valley.

Though some local firms may offer lower prices than Avis, Budget, Europcar and Hertz, these international agencies are more likely to let you return the car elsewhere in the country at no extra cost. The best deals can usually be found online or through the airline you are using to reach Vienna. The average daily hire charge for a medium-sized car is between €30–€50.

Third-party insurance is compulsory, but full cover is recommended. To avoid unpleasant surprises, make sure the price quoted includes all the necessary insurance and taxes. To hire a car, you must show your driving licence (held for at least a year) and passport. You also need a major credit card, or a large deposit will be required. The minimum age for renting cars ranges from 20 to 23.

Avis, tel: 7007 32700, www.avis.at
Budget, tel: 0810 500 501, www.budget.at
Megadrive, tel: 501 054120, www.megadrive.at
Europcar, tel: 01-866 16, www.europcar.at
Hertz, tel: 01-795 32, www.hertz.at

I'd like to rent a car **Ich möchte bitte ein Auto mieten**
today **für heute**
tomorrow **für morgen**
for a week **für eine Woche**

CLIMATE

Spring is Vienna's most pleasant season. Chestnut trees and white lilacs are in blossom for the city's music festival. In July and August the Viennese leave the city relatively free for visitors, and in autumn, the Wienerwald is in splendid colour for the *Heuriger* wine gardens, and the opera and theatre season in the city centre. Even in winter Vienna is worth the trip for a marvellous white Christmas, despite the cold east wind.

The chart shows Vienna's average monthly temperatures:

	J	F	M	A	M	J	J	A	S	O	N	D
°F	30	34	41	50	59	64	68	66	61	50	41	34
°C	-1	1	5	10	15	18	20	19	16	10	5	1

CLOTHING (Kleidung)

To best prepare for the extremes of Vienna's weather, take light cottons for the very hot summer afternoons and your warmest woollen layers for the bitter winter. The wind off the steppe can whip through at any time; so even in the middle of the summer, for an occasional cool evening, take a sweater and raincoat. The Viennese like to dress up for the theatre, concerts and opera, but a dark suit or cocktail dress is nearly always appropriate. A dinner jacket or evening dress may be worn on very special occasions, such as for premieres and galas.

CRIME AND SAFETY (See also Emergencies and Police)

Austria is a rather convention-bound society and the level of crime, though rising, is less than in some comparable countries. Nevertheless, all the usual precautions should be taken whilst travelling in a foreign country: valuables should ideally be left in a safe provided at the hotel and the interiors of parked cars should be cleared of tempting objects. You should carry some sort of ID on your person at all times, and it is a good idea to make a photocopy of your passport and have a record of the numbers of your credit, and any other, cards in case of loss or theft. Report thefts and incidents to the police (Polizei) who are generally very helpful to visitors from Western countries.

I want to report a theft. **Ich möchte einen Diebstahl melden.**

D

DISABLED TRAVELLERS

Vienna has implemented a great many schemes to enable wheelchair access. Most hotels have wheelchair access and some have rooms adapted for disabled people, though it would be wise to question the manager before making a reservation, to ensure that the room is suitable. Older buses and trams are not accessible, though many U-Bahn stations are. The Vienna Tourist Board (www.wien.info) can provide up-to-date information and has a list of sights and attractions with wheelchair access – the Riesenrad (Ferris wheel) is accessible. Local voluntary organisations may also offer help.

Fahrtendienst Haas, Karl Schäferstrasse 6, A-1210, tel: 27700, www.members.aon.at/haas-bus, provides transport for wheelchair users.

DRIVING (See also Car Rental/Hire)

To bring your car into Austria you will need:

valid driving licence (national licence for Europeans);

car registration papers;

national identity sticker for your car;

red warning triangle in case of breakdown;

first-aid kit;

reflective jacket.

Road conditions are by and large very good in Austria, only remote country roads are not paved.

Driving regulations. Drive on the right, pass on the left. Although drivers in Austria follow the same basic rules which apply in other countries that drive on the right, there are some rules that might differ somewhat:

On the motorway *(Autobahn)* passing another vehicle on its right is prohibited.

Vehicles coming from the right have priority at crossroads without other signals.

Trams have priority, even when coming from the left.

You must wear seat-belts.

Children under the age of 12 may not sit in the front, and must use a special safety seat.

It is prohibited to use your horn (day or night) in town.

Vehicles must halt behind trams when they are slowing down to stop and when loading or unloading passengers.

Drink-driving is a very serious offence in Austria. The permissible alcohol level in the blood is 0.5 percent.

---

driving licence **Führerschein**
car registration papers **Zulassungsschein**
green card **Grüne Karte**
Where's the nearest car park, please? **Wo ist der nächste Parkplatz, bitte?**
Can I park here? **Darf ich hier parken?**
Are we on the right road for...? **Sind wir auf der richtigen Strasse nach...?**
Check the oil/tyres/battery, please. **Öl/Reifen/Batterie prüfen, bitte.**
I've had a breakdown. **Ich habe eine Panne.**
There's been an accident. **Es ist ein Unfall passiert.**

Speed limits. On motorways (expressways) 130kmh (81mph) or 100kmh (62mph); on other roads 100kmh or 80kmh (50mph); in built-up areas 50kmh (31mph); with caravan (trailer) 80kmh (50mph) on the open road; with studded tyres 100kmh (62mph) on motorways, 80kmh (50mph) on other roads.

Parking. In streets with tram tracks, parking is prohibited from 8pm to 5am from mid-December to the end of March for snow clearance. If at all possible, use public transport within the Gürtel (outer ring road) since one-way streets and traffic jams add confusion within the city, where there is a lack of parking space. To park in 'blue' zones you will need parking tickets, valid from 8am to 6pm for up to 90 minutes. Tickets are available in banks and tobacco shops *(Tabaktrafik)*.

Breakdowns. The warning triangle must be displayed to indicate a broken-down vehicle and hazard lights must be switched on. Assistance can be obtained by calling the ÖAMTC (Austrian Automobile Club), tel: 120, or ARBÖ (Austrian Drivers' Association), tel: 123. Accidents involving injury must be reported to the police.

Anfang (Parking) Start
Ausfahrt Exit
Aussicht Viewpoint
Bau-arbeiten Road works
Einbahn-strasse One way
Ende (Parking) End
Fahrbahn-wechsel Change lanes
Fussgänger Pedestrians
Gefahr Danger
Geradeaus Straight on
Glatteis Slippery roads
Halten-verboten No stopping
Licht einschalten Use headlights
Ortsende Town ends
Parken erlaubt Parking allowed
Rechts, links einbiegen Turn right, left
Rollsplitt Loose gravel
Sackgasse No through road
Spital Hospital

Steinschlag Falling stones
Umleitung Diversion
Vorfahrt Priority
Vorsicht Caution
Werktags von 7 bis 17 Uhr Weekdays 7am to 5pm
Zufahrt gestattet Entrance permitted

E

ELECTRICITY

You'll need an adapter for most British and US plugs: Austrian sockets have round holes. Electricity supplies are 220 volt, and US equipment will require a transformer. Shaver outlets are generally dual voltage.

EMBASSIES AND CONSULATES

Contact your consulate or embassy only for real emergencies, such as loss of a passport or all your money, a serious accident or trouble with the police.

Australia: Mattiellistrasse 2, 1040 Vienna, tel: 01-506 740, www.austria.embassy.gov.au

Canada: Laurenzerberg 2, 1010 Vienna; tel: 01-531 383 000; www.canadainternational.gc.ca

Ireland: Rotenturmstrasse 16–18, 1010 Vienna; tel: 01-715 4246; www.embassyofireland.at

New Zealand: Mattiellistrasse 2-4/3, 1040 Vienna; tel: 01-505 3021; www.nzembassy.com/austria

South Africa: Sandgasse 33, 1190 Vienna; tel: 01-320 6493; www.suedafrika-botschaft.at

UK: Jauresgasse 12, 1030 Vienna; tel: 01-716 130; http://ukinaustria.fco.gov.uk

US: Boltzmanngasse 16, 1090 Vienna; tel: 01-313 390; http://austria.usembassy.gov/

EMERGENCIES (See also Crime and Safety and Police)

In an emergency the pan-European emergency number **120** should be called.

The following are the old numbers for the various emergency services that also still work.

Police **133**

Fire **122**

Ambulance **144**

I need a doctor/dentist. **Ich brauche einen Arzt/ Zahnarzt.**

ambulance **Krankenwagen**

Fire! **Feuer!**

Help! **Hilfe!**

hospital **Spital**

police **Polizei**

G

GAY AND LESBIAN TRAVELLERS

This sophisticated capital has a relatively friendly attitude towards the gay and lesbian community. Since 1996, the Regenbogen (Gay Rainbow) Parade has been held every June on the Ringstrasse.

A list of restaurants, hotels and bars which welcome gays and lesbians is provided at many websites, including www.vienna.gaycities.com, www.travelgayeurope.com/gay-map-of-vienna and www.patroc.com/vienna.

Two places for information are: Heumühlgasse 14/1, 1040 Vienna, tel: 01-216 6604, www.hosiwien.at, and Rosa Lila Villa, 6, Linke Wienzeile 102, tel: 01-586 8150, www.villa.at. A 'Gay and Lesbian Guide for Vienna' is available for download from the city's tourism website, www.wien.info.

GETTING THERE

By Air: There is regular service to Vienna from various centres in the UK. Austrian Airlines (www.aua.com) operates scheduled flights from Heathrow and Stansted and British Airways (www.ba.com) from Heathrow and Gatwick. Flying time from London is two and a half hours. The low-cost airline easyJet (www.easyjet.com) flies from Gatwick and Luton to Vienna, while both easyJet and Ryanair (www.ryanair.com) operate a service to Salzburg. The train journey from Salzburg to Vienna takes three hours. Ryanair also fly to Bratislava in Slovakia, a short hop across the border from Vienna.

In addition to non-stop flights from New York and Chicago, there is a scheduled service from more than 40 American cities as well as a dozen cities in Canada to European gateway destinations from which you can make connections to Vienna.

By Car: The quickest route to Vienna from the UK is via Calais through Brussels, Cologne, Nuremburg, Passau and Linz (1300km (800 miles), although there are more attractive routes, such as Die Romantische Strasse (the Romantic Road), via Rothenburg ob der Tauber, through the countryside. There are regular daily car ferry departures from Dover to Calais, or you can put your car on the train and travel through the Channel Tunnel from Folkestone to Calais in 35 minutes.

Depending from which direction you come, you might be able to put your car on the train for part of the journey. In the summer a car-train (Autozug) service links Vienna with cities in Germany and Italy. Arriving with the car-train allows you to avoid traffic jams around Vienna and brings you close to the town centre.

The Austrian Federal Railways (www.oebb.at) operates car-trains between Vienna and Bischofshofen, Feldkirch (overnight service with couchettes also available), Linz, Villach and Innsbruck and Salzburg (both during the ski season only).

By Coach: For details of coach services to Vienna from London and other European cities contact Eurolines (www.eurolines. co.uk).

By Train: The Köln–Vienna sleeper (book online at www.bahn.de) is the easiest way to reach Austria from London (connect via Brussels on Eurostar) and it takes about 13 hours; the entire trip, London to Vienna, takes about 20 hours. The cabins are very comfortable and couchettes are also available. Book online at (www.bahn.de).

The Austrian National Railpass (Bundes-Netzkarte) allows unlimited travel on Austrian Railways for one month. Contact Austrian Federal Railways for details (www.oebb.at).

GUIDES AND TOURS *(Fremdenführer; Rundfahrten)*

The most romantic tour of Vienna is in the famous horse-drawn *Fiaker* cab. These are usually parked at the Heldenplatz, Stephansplatz, or near the Albertina and will take you around the major sightseeing spots. Make sure you agree on the cost of the trip before you begin.

Vienna Sightseeing bus tours, with English commentary, are conveniently run on a hop-on/hop-off basis on five sightseeing routes with up to 45 stops. Buy tickets (from €13.50) online at www. viennasightseeing.at.

The Tourist Information Board organises guided **theme tours on foot** (*Wiener Spaziergänge*, www.wienguide.at), often with English-speaking guides. Each tour lasts approximately 90 minutes. They cover all manner of special interests: Medieval Vienna, Hundertwasser and modern architecture, Jewish Vienna, *Jugendstil*, the *Musikmeile* (Music Mile) a classical music walk, and *Der Dritte Mann* (The Third Man), which follows in the footsteps of the classic 1949 film. Most hotels can arrange – at a price – for English-speaking guides or interpreters to accompany you on your way around the city. Otherwise contact the Vienna Tourist Board for more information or **Vienna Guide Service**, www.guides-in-vienna.at.

We'd like an English-speaking guide. **Wir möchten einen englisch-sprachigen Fremdenführer.**
I need an English interpreter. **Ich brauche einen Dolmetscher für Englisch.**
How long will the ride take? **Wie lange dauert die Fahrt?**
What does it cost? **Was kostet es?**

H

HEALTH AND MEDICAL CARE *(Ärztliche Hilfe)*

No special precautions need to be taken when travelling to Austria, which is generally a very safe, clean and healthy country with excellent medical services. Emergency medical care is free of charge for EU citizens, though you may have to pay for medicines. Before travelling, British subjects should obtain a free European Health Insurance Card (forms available at post offices, online at www.ehic.org.uk, or tel: 0845 606 2030). Citizens of countries outside the EU should ensure that they are covered by a comprehensive private health insurance policy. Such insurance is worth considering in any case in order to cover any longer-term problems and to ensure prompt repatriation if necessary. Minor health problems can often be dealt with by visiting a pharmacy *(Apotheke)*. These sport a green cross and/or snake and staff sign. In big cities several stay open all night and the addresses should be posted in the windows of those that close. The website www.wien-vienna.com/nachtapotheken.php lists all-night pharmacies. In case of accident or serious illness, call the ambulance service on **144** or general emergency number **120**.

Where is there a pharmacy on duty? **Wo ist die diensthabende Apotheke?**

L

LANGUAGE

Austria is German-speaking, but English is also very widely understood and spoken. The *Berlitz German Phrase Book and Dictionary* covers most situations you're likely to encounter in Austria.

M

MAPS

The Tourist Information Board gives away excellent street-maps of the city. Most useful will always be a large-scale map of the Innere Stadt (Inner City) and of the U-Bahn network.

MEDIA

Major hotels and most kiosks in the First District sell English-language daily newspapers from London, *International Herald Tribune*, *Wall Street Journal* and *USA Today*, and the news magazines.

TV in the major hotels usually has CNN and BBC World news services, along with other major European channels. The state-run broadcaster for TV and radio is ÖRF (www.orf.at).

MONEY *(Geld)*

The euro (€) is the official currency used in Austria. Notes are denominated in 5, 10, 20, 50, 100 and 500 euros (last two rarely seen); coins in 1 and 2 euros and 1, 2, 5, 10, 20 and 50 cents.

Changing money. The easiest way to obtain euros is with a suitable debit/credit card at a cash machine *(Geldautomat)*, but note that not all cards are accepted at all machines and that most banks charge for this service. Foreign currency can be changed at practically any bank or savings bank *(Sparkasse)*. As well as bureaux de change, travel agencies and hotels will often change money, though the rate is not likely to be a favourable one. Travellers' cheques are widely accepted but probably not worth the hassle for the protection they provide.

Credit cards. Major credit cards are widely but not universally accepted, least of all in small establishments. Cash still rules in Austria, but you should be able to settle your hotel bill using your credit/debit card. Occasionally you may come across an establishment that only takes one type of card.

> I want to change some pounds/dollars **Ich möchte Pfund/ Dollar wechseln.**
> Do you accept travellers' cheques? **Nehmen Sie Reiseschecks an?**
> Where's the nearest ATM, please? **Wo ist der nächste Geldautomat, bitte?**

O

OPENING HOURS

Banks. Monday to Friday 8am–3pm, possibly with later opening on Thursday.

Museums. Most museums open at 9am or 10am and close at 5pm or 6pm, though there may be late opening on one day a week. Many are closed all day Monday. See individual listings in the Where to Go section.

Post offices. Monday to Friday 8am–6pm.

Shops. Official shop opening hours are Monday to Friday 9am–6pm with early closing on Saturday. Small shops close at lunchtime while larger establishments may open earlier and stay open longer one evening a week. In areas frequented by large groups of tourists, however, shops may remain open as long as there is a chance of custom. Shops located at airports and main railway stations keep longer hours.

P

POLICE (*Polizei*, see also Crime and Safety and Emergencies)

Vienna's police wear green caps and jackets with black trousers, and drive white cars. Traffic police wear white caps and, in summer, white jackets. Street parking is supervised by Politessen (traffic wardens) in blue jackets and white hats. If you are fined for any reason, the police have the right to ask you to pay on the spot. In emergencies, call **133** or **112**. Vienna's main police station is at Schottenring 7-9.

Where is the nearest police station, please? **Wo ist die nächste Polizei-wache, bitte?**

POST OFFICE (*Postamt*)

Apart from regular post office hours (Monday–Friday 8am–6pm), post offices at main railway stations (Westbahnhof, Südbahnhof and Franz Josefs-Bahnhof) are open day and night. Other offices offering this 24-hour service for registered, air and express mail (with a small extra charge): Central Post Office, Fleischmarkt 19, and Central Telegraph Office, Börseplatz 1. Letterboxes and post office signs are coloured yellow.

express (special delivery) **Express/Eilbote**
airmail **Luftpost**
A stamp for this letter/postcard, please. **Eine Marke für diesen Brief/diese Postkarte, bitte.**

PUBLIC HOLIDAYS (*Feiertage*)

1 January *Neujahr* New Year's Day
6 January *Dreikönigstag* Epiphany

March/April *Ostermontag* Easter Monday
1 May *Tag der Arbeit* May Day/Labour Day
May/June *Christi Himmelfahrt* Ascension Day
May/June *Pfingstmontag* Whit Monday
June *Fronleichnam* Corpus Christi
15 August *Mariä Himmelfahrt* Assumption Day
26 October *Nationalfeiertag* National Day
1 November *Allerheiligen* All Saints Day
8 December *Maria Empfägnis* Immaculate Conception
25 December *Weihnachtsfeiertag* Christmas Day
26 December *Weihnachtsfeiertag (2)* St Stephen's Day

T

TELEPHONES

To call Vienna from abroad, dial 0043 followed by the area code (1) and the number.

To make an international call from Austria, dial 00 followed by the country code, area code and number.

Within Austria, to make a call from Vienna to another dial the relevant area code starting with zero, then the subscriber number. You do not need the area code when dialling within the same city/code area.

Local SIM cards are inexpensive and as Austria is a member of the EU, roaming charges are low. Rather than cash, most public telephones take phonecards, available from post offices and tobacconists.

TIME ZONE

Austria follows Central European Time (GMT +1 hour) and in summer an hour is added for daylight saving.

See the box opposite to compare the time in Vienna with other cities in the world.

New York	London	**Vienna**	Jo'burg	Sydney	Auckland
6am	11am	**noon**	noon	8pm	10pm

TIPPING

Although a service charge is included in restaurant bills, it is customary to round the amount up to the nearest euro or round figure. A small sum is also expected by cloakroom attendants, porters, chambermaids and tour guides.

TOILETS

Well-maintained public toilets can usually be found in tourist hotspots and at railway stations. Keep small change handy in case there is a charge. Men's toilets are marked with the word 'Herren', Ladies with 'Damen'.

TOURIST INFORMATION

The Austrian National Tourist Office (ANTO) dispenses comprehensive information both on the internet and in brochure form about where to go, what to see and where to stay and eat out in Vienna (and other Austrian cities). Visit the website at www.austria.info for more details. Offices are closed to the public but brochures can be ordered from the following ANTO offices (contact during business hours, 9am–5pm):

Australia: email: info@antosyd.org.au; tel: (2) 9299 3621.

Canada: email: travel@austria.info; tel: 416 967-3381.

Ireland: email: holiday@austria.info; tel: 189 0930118.

UK: email: london@austria.info; tel: 20-3409 6616.

US: email: travel@austria.info; tel: (212) 944 68 80.

Vienna Tourist Board. The Tourist Information Office is conveniently located right behind the Vienna State Opera at Albertinaplatz 1/corner of Maysedergasse, tel: 24 555, www.wien.info, open 9am–7pm daily.

TRANSPORT

Maps for Vienna's excellent public transport system (buses, trams and underground rail) are available at main stops as well as at the central public transport information offices at Karlsplatz and Stephansplatz.

Tickets *(Karten)* can be bought from a conductor or a machine on trams and buses, from the booking office or a machine for mainline or city trains. A single ticket for a journey by tram, bus and underground, which covers changes made without interruption, costs €2.20. Tickets can be bought in advance from a tobacconist's *(Tabaktrafik)* or transport offices *(Verkehrsbetriebe)*. Travel passes are available for 24 hours (€7.60) and 72 hours (€16.50). For detailed tariff information, timetables, routes etc., see www.wienerlinien.at.

Where is the nearest bus/tram stop, please? **Wo ist die nächste Bus-/Strassenbahn-Haltestelle, bitte?**
I want a ticket to ... **Ich will eine Fahrkarte nach ...**
single/return **einfache Fahrt/Rückfahrkarte**

V

VISAS AND ENTRY REQUIREMENTS

A valid passport is required for entry. Visitors from European Union (EU) countries, including the US, Canada, Australia and New Zealand do not require a visa, but nationals of other countries that do not have a reciprocal agreement with Austria do. For more information check www.bmeia.gv.at/london.

W

WEBSITES AND INTERNET ACCESS

Wi-fi is available at most hotels of any standard but is not free as often as it is in the UK. Internet cafés are virtually a thing of the past in Austria. If you are taking your laptop along, consider purchasing a cheap local 'dongle' to access the internet anywhere there is a mobile phone signal. These can cost as little as €20 and even the lowest download speeds are fast enough for general browsing.

Useful websites:

www.wien.info One-stop shop for Vienna visitor information.

www.austria.info The Austrian Tourist Board site.

www.wien.gv.at The City of Vienna's website, lists information on all aspects of life in the city and is available in English.

www.wienmuseum.at For city museums.

www.austrianews.co.uk Up-to-date news from Austria.

www.inyourpocket.com/austria/vienna Expat restaurant, bar, hotel and entertainment reviews.

Y

YOUTH HOSTELS *(Jugendherberge)*

For details of organised youth hostels in Vienna, contact: Öster-reichischer Jugendherbergsverband (Austrian Youth Hostels Association), 1010 Vienna, Schottenring 28, tel: 01-5333 5353, www.oejhv.or.at. Vienna also has a few independent backpacker hostels which can be booked through sites such as www.hostelworld.com and www.hostelbookers.com.

Vienna Youth Hostels:

Jugendherberge Wien Myrthengasse – Myrthengasse 7, tel: 01-523 63160; hostel@chello.at; Dorm beds from €19.

Jugendgästehaus Brigittenau – Adalbert Stifter Strasse 73, tel: 01-332 8294; jgh.1200wien@chello.at; Dorm beds from €19.

Wombats City Hostel – The Lounge – Mariahilfer Strasse 137, tel: 01-897 2336; www.wombats-hostels.com; Dorm beds from €13.

Hostel Ruthensteiner – Robert Hamerling Gasse 24, tel: 01-893 4202; www.hostelruthensteiner.com; Dorm beds from €10.

RECOMMENDED HOTELS

Vienna's hotels easily compare in quality to those of other major European capitals. However, a slight shortage of accommodation, particularly during peak season – Christmas and New Year, and from Easter to the end of September – does mean that advance booking is advisable. Reservations can be made online and by telephone (country code 43 followed by area code 1), and are binding even if not confirmed in writing. Vienna's hotels used to be heavy on the frump, frill and the Biedermeier look, and while this is still prominent, in recent years a number of smart design hotels have opened up, lending a more contemporary vibe to the city's accommodation scene.

The hotels listed here are placed in four categories based on the approximate price in euros per night for a double room with private bath or shower unless otherwise stated. A service charge and taxes are included in the price. Breakfast is generally included in the rate, though it's best to check when you reserve as it is not always the case in pricier establishments, and this is usually a buffet of various cold meats and cheeses, cereals, bread, rolls, jam and coffee. Always confirm prices when booking. All the hotels listed take major credit cards; wheelchair access is widespread but not ubiquitous.

The district number precedes the street address.

€€€€	over 300 euros
€€€	200–300 euros
€€	120–200 euros
€	under 120 euros

THE INNERE STADT (DISTRICT 1)

Arenberg €€ *1, Stubenring 2, tel: 01-512 5291,* www.arenberg.at. The doyen among pensions (part of the Best Western group), set in an atmospheric Ringstrasse building with a plush, elegant atmosphere and excellent location. Popular with visiting actors and singers, whose photographs adorn the reception area, all rooms have satellite TV and direct-dial telephones, and breakfast is included in the room rate.

Astoria €€€ *1, Kärntnerstrasse 32–34, tel: 01-515 7788, www. austria-trend.at.* A civilised and venerable old hotel immediately behind the Staatsoper. The 128 bedrooms are generously cut and comfortable with traditional décor. Some of them are accessible to disabled guests.

Hotel Austria €€ *1, Am Fleischmarkt 20, tel: 01-515 23, www.hotel austria-wien.at.* Well maintained rooms in a very centrally placed hotel; those without bath are cheaper but all have free Wi-fi. A smart, friendly and tranquil retreat right in the city centre.

Bristol €€€€ *1, Kärntner Ring 1, tel: 01-515 160, www.bristolvienna. com.* An Art Nouveau building dating from 1884 providing a bit more cosiness than many other five-star hotels. Its restaurant, the Korso, is known for its light Viennese cuisine and distinguished wine list. There are non-smoking rooms and wheelchair facilities for guests.

Do & Co €€€€ *1, Stephansplatz 12, tel: 01-24 188, www.doco.com.* This über-chic design hotel may just occupy the best spot of any Vienna hotel, on the upper storeys of the Haas Haus opposite the Stephansdom. Impeccable service and amazing views from the Bang & Olufsen-equipped cool, minimalist rooms are complimented by one of the most popular bars (the Onyx) and restaurants in the city. Although the rack rates are pretty high, you may get a good deal in low season.

Hollman Beletage €€ *1, Köllnerhofgasse 6, tel: 01-961 1960, www. hollmann-beletage.at.* It is hard to recommend this small (25 rooms) hotel enough. It's super-central, and the rooms are contemporary and chic in their design and commendably well kept. The vibe is laid back and the reception even shuts down at night, leaving the guests to help themselves at the bar. Excellent value, and a hearty break-fast included in the price.

Imperial €€€€ *1, Kärntner Ring 16, tel: 01-501 100, www.imperial vienna.com.* Official guests of state, actors and leading pop stars bed down at the Imperial, with its 138 stylish rooms and suites. Definitely the place to be seen, and the restaurant is one of the best and most expensive in town (the café isn't bad either). All rooms can accommodate guests in wheelchairs.

König von Ungarn €€€ *1, Schulerstrasse 10, tel: 01-515 840,* www.kvu.at. Centrally located only metres from the Stephansdom, and over 400 years old, this hotel is packed with old-fashioned charm. It has everything you would expect of a four-star hotel, and the glass-roofed inner courtyard is particularly attractive. All rooms are wheelchair-friendly and there's free Wi-Fi throughout.

Mailbergerhof €€ *1, Annagasse 7, tel: 01-512 0641,* www.mailbergerhof.at. This old building once belonged to the Knights Hospitallers but today boasts a 21st-century interior. Located in the pedestrian area of the city centre. Breakfast is included in the room rate.

Meridien €€€€ *1, Opernring 13, tel: 01-588 900,* www.starwoodhotels.com. Five-star luxury in a row of converted Ringstrasse buildings. The interiors have been beautifully designed, with clean modern lines. The restaurants come highly recommended as well.

Nossek €€ *1, Graben 17, tel: 01-533 7041,* www.pension-nossek.at. Small, cosy 30-room pension in the heart of Vienna's shopping district. Credit cards are not accepted and reservations are highly recommended in the high season. For longer stays ask about the pension's apartment.

Palais Coburg €€€€ *1, Coburgbastei 4, tel: 01-518 18,* www.palais-coburg.at. Wallet-stretchingly expensive but wonderfully opulent, this mid-19th-century palace has been converted into a series of luxury suites. Everything is, as you would expect, very suave, with a fine-dining restaurant, pool and city centre garden.

Park Hyatt Vienna €€€€ *1, Am Hof 2, tel: 01-227 401 234,* www.parkhyattvienna.com. A luxurious hotel in a 100-year-old listed building with marble floors, alabaster and shiny brass. 143 opulent rooms, including 35 suites and three accessible rooms. Facilities include a spa, sauna, fitness centre and an indoor pool. Excellent restaurant, the Bank.

Pertschy €€ *1, Habsburgergasse 5, tel: 01-534 49,* www.pertschy.com. A friendly small hotel right in the middle of the Innere Stadt. The rooms are very comfy and pleasant in a kitschy Viennese sort of way (which is all part of the charm) and breakfast is included in the price.

Radisson Blu Style Hotel €€€ *1, Herrengassse 12, tel: 01-227 800*, www.radissonblu.com. Very central, chic and well-designed, this 21st-century 'style' hotel is a swish place to stay. The rooms are very comfortable and the facilities excellent. It's also not quite as expensive as it first appears (check out the web 'specials').

The Ring €€€ *1, Kärntner Ring 8, tel: 01-22 122*, www.theringhotel.com. Opened in 2007, this cool but comfy Ringstrasse hotel has been given an intimate designer interior. The good-value classy rooms have a gently modern look, there is a great bar with a geographically roving wine list, and the hotel has a good day spa with the usual facials and massages.

Sacher €€€€ *1, Philharmonikerstrasse 4, tel: 01-514 560*, www.sacher.com. Archdukes, ministers and senior army officers used to stay here, and the Sacher is still the city's most famous hotel. Past its heyday, perhaps, but you can still be sure of top-class service. Some of the 149 rooms are accessible to wheelchair users.

Suzanne € *1, Walfischgasse 4, tel: 01-513 2507*, www.pension-suzanne.at. Two generations of the Strafinger family have worked to provide homely digs in their spacious apartments with *fin-de-siècle*-style furnishings. The pension is close to the Opera and city centre.

Topazz €€€ *1, Lichtensteg 3, tel: 01-532 2250*, www.hoteltopazz.com. Occupying a striking building with oval portholes for windows, this cutting edge hotel takes the design theme to new heights. Bedrooms are studies in cool styling, all blacks and beiges, quirky lamps and big-print wallpaper – and you can perch in those funky windows to admire the views across town. Enjoy a health-conscious start to the day in the futuristic breakfast room.

Wandl €€–€€€ *1, Petersplatz 9, tel: 01-534 550*, www.hotel-wandl.com. Located immediately behind the Peterskirche (just off Graben), and thus very much at the hub of things. It was built in the 1700s as the residence of a court official, and still retains a historic feel. The rooms are surprisingly contemporary and rates are reasonable for the facilities on offer.

Zur Wiener Staatsoper €€ *1, Krugerstrasse 11, tel: 01-5131 274,* www.zurwienerstaatsoper.at. As the name suggests, this popular choice is close to the opera. Small rooms, most with en-suite facilities, all facing a quiet, residential street. Advance reservations are recommended.

AROUND THE RINGSTRASSE (DISTRICTS 2–9)

Altstadt Vienna €€–€€€ *7, Kirchengasse 41, tel: 01-5226 666,* www. altstadt.at. Housed in a 19th-century apartment block, attentive staff, cutting edge décor and a location within walking distance of most sights make this a sure-fire winner. Room rates include breakfast and afternoon tea, a feature you won't find many other places. Rooms are in converted apartments with tall windows, double doors and preposterously high ceilings.

Das Triest €€€ *4, Wiedner Hauptstrasse 12, tel: 01-589 180,* www.das triest.at. This great little design hotel set the scene for the explosion of chic, contemporary places to sleep in the Austrian capital. An old stable, dating back approximately 300 years, was given a brand new look by designer Terence Conran producing a characteristic mix of beautifully lit minimalist rooms and restored elements of the original building. There is also a decent Italian restaurant and a great bar.

Das Tyrol €€–€€€ *6, Mariahilfer Strasse 15, tel: 01-587 5415,* www. das-tyrol.at. Located in the Museumsquartier, this boutique hotel has brightly decorated rooms, pristine bathrooms and a breakfast you'll be looking forward to the night before. The hotel is littered with pieces of contemporary art to get you in the mood for Vienna's many museums and galleries.

Haydn € *6, Mariahilfer Strasse 57–59, tel: 01-5874 4140,* www.haydn-hotel.at. This simple, mid-range pension is located in a noisy area, but is only a few minutes from the city centre by U-Bahn. There is cycle storage space available to guests, and breakfast is included in the reasonable price.

The Imperial Riding School €€€ *3, Ungargasse 60, tel: 01-711 750,* www.marriott.com. One of the city's architecturally most striking hotels converted from riding stables built in 1850. It is slightly off the beaten track, about 10 minutes by tram from the Ringstrasse. All the comfortable but simple rooms can accommodate wheelchair users. As well as a lavish reception area there is an inviting indoor pool.

Kugel € *7, Siebensterngasse 43, tel: 01-5233 355,* www.hotelkugel.at. Good location in the middle of the shopping district, and small, clean rooms. Enthusiastic owners make the experience more enjoyable. Some rooms are equipped for wheelchair use.

Levante Parliament €€€–€€€€ *8, Auerspergstrasse 9, tel: 01-228 280,* www.thelevante.com. A fantastic design hotel just behind the Parliament, parallel to the Ringstrasse. Set in a building from 1908, originally designed by Secession architect Robert Oerley, the 2006 redesign featuring chic and cosy reds, browns and oranges, as well as specially commissioned photographs by Curt Themessl and glass sculptures by Ioan Nemtoi (for sale if you take a fancy to them), blends in well with the original fabric of the building. The rooms and bathrooms themselves are studies in comfort and understated elegance and the lovely interior courtyard is a great spot for a drink or meal from the hotel's Nemtoi restaurant. In the basement is a soothing sauna and 'wellness' area.

Hotel Rathaus Wien €€€ *8, Lange Gasse 13, tel: 01-400 1122,* www.hotel-rathaus-wien.at. Quiet rooms right in the middle of the lively Josefstadt district, with its many small bars. Each of the well-designed rooms is named after an Austrian wine maker, and samples of their wines are found in the minibar. Rates tumble in winter.

Wild € *8, Lange Gasse 10, tel: 01-4065 174,* www.pension-wild.com. A popular pension in the Josefstadt district with large modern and very clean rooms with or without en suite facilities, leading off a central stairwell. There are kitchenettes on every floor for light meals and a decent breakfast (included in the price) is served on the ground floor. A welcoming place to stay for gay and lesbian visitors.

Zipser €–€€ *8, Lange Gasse 49, tel: 01-404 540,* www.zipser.at. In a rather grand, century-old building, this attractive pension has been run with great care by the same family for three generations. Rooms facing the garden are slightly more expensive. Just beyond the Ring in the interesting Josefstadt district, a few minutes' walk from the Rathaus and the Inner City.

FURTHER AFIELD

Klimt €€ *14, Felbigergasse 58, tel: 01-914 5565*, www.klimt-hotel.at. Renovated in a neo-*Jugendstil* style, this hotel offers the unusual option for guests to order special mattresses on request (a nice emphasis on a good night's sleep). It also has a fabulous honeymoon suite with canopied bed. Snack bar with meals available.

Landhaus Furhgassl-Huber €€ *19, Rathstrasse 24, tel: 01-440 3033*, www.landhaus-fuhrgassl-huber.at. This hotel is at Neustift am Walde, an area of vineyards and *Heuriger* within the city limits. Once the town hall, the fine interior was designed by Walter von Hoessl, one-time stage designer for the State Opera. It has comfortable rooms and is in a lovely, quiet location.

Parkhotel Schönbrunn €€€ *13, Hietzinger Hauptstrasse 12, tel: 01-878 040*, www.austria-trend.at. Very close to the palace and gardens of Schönbrunn, this recently renovated hotel formerly housed the emperor's guests and is still redolent of the Imperial past. Amenities include Wi-fi and satellite TV and some of the 312 rooms are wheelchair friendly. Rates include a generous breakfast.

The Rooms € *22, Schlenthergasse 17, tel: 0664-431 6830*, www.therooms.at. This lovely bed and breakfast is a little way out of the centre in Donaustadt (near to Kagran U-bahn). Just four rooms (for one to three people each), which are beautifully furnished, with views of the garden. Extremely good value but payment is in cash only.

Roomz € *11, Paragonstrasse 1, tel: 01-7431 777*, www.roomz-vienna.com. Excellent value for a bit of modern comfort, this budget hotel near the Gasometers has 152 spotless rooms with a designer feel, all with contemporary bathrooms attached. There is a pleasant 24-hour bar and restaurant as well.

Schild €€€ *19, Neustift am Walde 97–99, tel: 01-4404 0440,* www.hotel-schild.at. This 28-room hotel is a paradise for anyone who loves wine, since it is surrounded by *Heurigen.* The beautiful country location will also appeal to keen cyclists as the hotel offers both cycle storage and repair facilities. Some wheelchair-friendly rooms are available.

Sophienalpe € *14, Sofienalpenstrasse 13, tel: 01-486 2432,* www.sophienalpe.at. A country hotel, 20km (12 miles) from the centre, originally built by Franz Joseph as a summerhouse for his mother, Duchess Sophie. It offers good food, comfy rooms and a pool, and is an absolute bargain.

GUMPOLDSKIRCHEN

Krug € *Schulgasse 1, tel: 0699 131-47273,* www.hotel-krug.at. A simply-furnished affordable hotel with 20 rooms, each with en suite bathroom, 20km (12 miles) from Vienna. Breakfast is included in the price.

Hotel Turmhof €€ *Josef Schöffel Strasse 9, tel: 02252-607 333,* www.hotel-turmhof.at. This modern make-over of a pretty old building makes for attractive large rooms with spacious bathrooms. Most rooms have views over the surrounding vineyards and there is a great rooftop sauna.

Winzerhotel Vöhringer €€ *Wienerstrasse 26, tel: 02252-607 400,* www.winzerhotel.at. A very well-maintained small business hotel with spotless rooms decorated in a modern style. The bathrooms are large and there is a lovely courtyard to sit out in when the weather is pleasant. It is only five minutes' walk to the station for the train into Vienna.

INDEX

INSIGHT ⊙ GUIDES POCKET GUIDE

VIENNA

First Edition 2016

Editor: Kate Drynan
Author: Jack Altman
Head of Production: Rebeka Davies
Picture Editor: Paul Burton
Cartography Update: Carte
Update Production: AM Services
Photography Credits: Austria Tourism 15, 30, 46, 51, 78, 82, 86, 91; Britta Jaschinski/Apa Publications 6MC, 6ML, 7M, 7M, 9, 26, 35, 38, 41, 57, 57, 74, 80, 84, 89, 90, 99, 100, 102; Corbis 42; Dreamstime 22, 52, 65, 83; Fotolia 4TC, 4TL, 36, 37, 56, 64, 66, 77; Glyn Genin/Apa Publications 4MC, 4ML, 5MC, 8R, 9R, 29, 32, 48, 55, 61, 67, 68, 70, 71, 93; iStock 5T, 5MC, 5M, 6TL, 8L, 11, 13, 17, 19, 21, 24, 49, 50, 53, 72, 88, 95, 96, 98; Public domain 5M, 62; Shutterstock 6TL, 7T, 7TC; Vienna Tourist Board 5TC, 44, 45
Cover Picture: iStock

Distribution

UK, Ireland and Europe: Apa Publications (UK) Ltd; sales@insightguides.com
United States and Canada: Ingram Publisher Services; ips@ingramcontent.com
Australia and New Zealand: Woodslane; info@woodslane.com.au
Southeast Asia: Apa Publications (SN) Pte; singaporeoffice@insightguides.com
Hong Kong, Taiwan and China: Apa Publications (HK) Ltd; hongkongoffice@insightguides.com
Worldwide: Apa Publications (UK) Ltd; sales@insightguides.com

Special Sales, Content Licensing and CoPublishing
Insight Guides can be purchased in bulk quantities at discounted prices. We can create special editions, personalised jackets and corporate imprints tailored to your needs. sales@insightguides.com; www.insightguides.biz

Contact us
Every effort has been made to provide accurate information in this publication, but changes are inevitable. The publisher cannot be responsible for any resulting loss, inconvenience or injury. We would appreciate it if readers would call our attention to any errors or outdated information. We also welcome your suggestions; please contact us at: hello@insightguides.com
www.insightguides.com

Vienna Transport